Bo...
by ...

Professional Breeders Series®

E C O

© 2007 by ECO Herpetological Publishing & Distribution.

ISBN 978-0-9788979-1-8

No part of this book may be reproduced or utilized in any form or by any means, electronic or mechanical, including photocopying, recording, or by any information storage or retrieval systems, without permission in writing from the publisher.

Copies available from:

ECO Herpetological Publishing & Distribution
915 Seymour Ave. Lansing, MI 48906 USA
telephone: 517.487.5595   fax: 517.371.2709
email: ecoorders@hotmail.com   website: http://www.reptileshirts.com

T-Rex Products, Inc.
http://t-rexproducts.com

Zoo Book Sales
http://www.zoobooksales.com

LIVING ART publishing
http://www.livingartpublishing.com

Cutting Edge Herpetological, Inc.
http://www.cuttingedgeherp.com

All photography by the author unless otherwise noted.

Design and layout by Russ Gurley.
Cover design by Rafael Porrata.

Printed in China.

Front Cover: A beautiful Hypomelanistic Nicaraguan Boa. Photo by Vin Russo.
Back Cover: A Coral Snow Boa, one of the most sought-after of all morphs. Photo by Vin Russo.

Boas

Boas

TABLE OF CONTENTS

INTRODUCTION	1
Chapter ONE: Taxonomy	6
Chapter TWO: Boa Constrictors as Pets	13
Chapter THREE: Feeding	31
Chapter FOUR: Breeding Boa Constrictors	38
Chapter FIVE: GENETICS	52
Chapter SIX: Diseases, Parasites, and Disorders in *Boa constrictor*	58
The Subspecies of *Boa constrictor*	69
Bolivian Boas	70
True Red-tailed Boas	72
Central American Boas	74
Long-tailed Boas	89
Dominican Boas	91
Argentine Boas	93
St. Lucia Boas	95
Orton's Boas	97
Pearl Island Boas	99
C.I.T.E.S.	102
PHOTO GALLERY	105
SUGGESTED READING	108

INTRODUCTION

Boa constrictor constrictor from Brazil.

Growing up in suburban New York in the 70s it was not common to see a boa in a pet shop. I had to travel to the Bronx Zoo reptile house or the Staten Island Zoo to see these amazing creatures. But at the age of fifteen I worked in a pet shop and had my first encounters with boas. Even though the mass exportation of Colombian Boas (*Boa c. imperator*) from the wild was in its infancy, at that time boas would also occasionally be shipped with tropical fish shipments and bird shipments and would end up in pet stores. Most were *Boa c. imperator* but every once and a while they received a true Red tailed boa (*Boa c. constrictor*) and regarded it as a rarer phase and asked more money for them. Even the importers did not know exactly what they were as they most likely purchased them from an exporter that was selling tropical fish and didn't care where it was caught. Also, it could have been caught in one country and shipped up river to another country to sell with the fish or birds as an added money maker.

It was obvious to me that there was a difference in these boas but to almost everyone else, they were all the same thing – *Boa constrictor*. It was hard, to impossible, to find any books at the local library and I had no access to any scientific journals or papers on boas. At that time in the pet trade all boas were simply considered to be "*Boa constrictor*" whether they were from Mexico or Argentina – it didn't matter, they were all placed in the same category.

Oddly enough, even the word "Boa" in many languages means "Large Snake". (This is ironic considering most boa subspecies rarely reach 8 feet.) The *Boa constrictor* name therefore had been highly abused and along with it a stigma of size had been attached. The incomplete knowledge of this species was likely due to poor sampling over its large geographic range, which made it even more difficult for herpetologists to pursue a comprehensive study.

Even though the species *Boa constrictor* has been known to science since 1758, the sytematics of the species is still in a deplorable state and in need of updating. But today, with the internet, mitochondrial DNA testing, and global satellite positioning we can get a clearer picture and more information about these creatures and their specific native habitats and localities. It is for these reasons that I have made the research of *Boa constrictors* my life's work. As a young man I spent many hours with two local herpetologists, Dr. Robert Price and Samuel McDowell, talking about boa taxononomy and reading old copies of *Herpetologica* and *Copeia*. I studied the past herpetologists' descriptions of Boa subspecies and spent years studying shed skins and living specimens that my brother Paul and I imported from South America and Central America. I have spent the last 22 years observing boas, photographing boas, and observing their different breeding and feeding habits. I have traveled to Central America and South America (the natural range of these creatures) to see how they live and to try to recognize the different subspecies, their habitats, maximum sizes, and evolutionary differences.

This book was written to help educate herpetoculturists and hobbyists about all the different Boa constrictors. These complex snakes have the largest geographic range of any reptile on Earth, spanning two continents from the Sonoran Desert of Mexico to Argentina, South America, comprising a geographic range of over 6 million

Cloud Forest of Costa Rica.

square miles. Their habitats range from lowland desert oases to mountainous rainforests.

A few books have been written in the past that are intended for the general public and are written to educate hobbyists about the basics of maintenance and care of boas. However, they have mostly failed to illustrate the subtle and obvious differences in *Boa constrictor*. Boas were simply placed in a general group or species and the subspecies were not explained or misinformation was given.

I felt that it is important to explain the color morphs and pattern anomalies that occur in some of these subspecies. These appealing anomalies are the main reason that boas are getting so much attention these days. They have taken the *Boa constrictor* to another level in the pet industry and have attracted the attention of many herpetoculturists. I will also discuss the man made genetic combinations that have made boa breeding a very popular part of our hobby and how the *race* to create new morphs has catapulted the boa industry into the next millennium.

This book was written for those people that are passionate about keeping and breeding *Boa constrictor*s. Identification is the key if you want to be successful in keeping and breeding these serpents.

Think of it this way . . . it would be next to impossible to maintain a rainforest species in a dry desert setting or a semi-arid species under wet rainforest conditions.

And lastly - I also hope that this book will help the Boa enthusiast identify with accuracy the different subspecies so that these beautiful creatures can remain pure in bloodlines. I say this because in the past when it was more difficult to obtain boas and information about boas – breeders would simply breed their boas to whatever similar looking mates they could find. This has created some poor genetic material and animals that are virtually unidentifiable and useless in a successful locality breeding program.

I believe it is very important and cannot emphasize enough the importance of keeping bloodlines pure for the future of the particular subspecies or race you may be working with and the future of herpetoculture. Even in the scenario of color morphs and pattern anomalies, I find it important to selectively breed F generations to improve on a particular gene.

Some zoos have made the mistake of breeding animals such as Tigers to other Tigers of unknown locality, thus creating genetic junk that are now spayed or neutered and kept as display animals only. The zoos currently use a form of pedigree with family trees to identify certain localities of Tiger. This is being done in case one day these animals may be released into the wild. The same scenario could occur with certain *Boa constrictor* subspecies in that pure genetic material will be needed for potential release into the wild.

Rainforests, deserts, and even many small islands are being devastated by humans for monetary purposes at an alarming rate. Because of this, the future of *Boa constrictor* lies in the hands of responsible breeders and zoos. Although it would be very nice to someday release boas to the islands or rainforests from which they have been exterminated, the fact is that herpetologists, zoologists, and fish and wildlife agencies are more concerned with the introduction of

Hypomelanistic Panamanian Boa, *Boa constrictor imperator*.

diseases from captive animals to the wild populations and therefore frown upon the idea. The results could be catastrophic to other native fauna and flora. Therefore it's up to the responsible breeders to keep their known bloodlines pure so we can have pure-blooded locality boas to enjoy in the future. At this time the only action we can take to preserve the native species of insular and locality boas is to preserve their native habitat.

Who knows what the future holds? Zoos never thought they would be releasing captive Tigers into Asia, captive Timber Wolves into Yellowstone National Park, and captive-hatched Galapagos Tortoises onto Espanola Island. But they **have** released them and with **excellent** results. So you never know – there may be a day in the future when captive boas will be released into the wild where an extinct population once lived.

Vincent P. Russo

Chapter ONE: Taxonomy

Corn Island Boa, *Boa constrictor imperator*.

Systematics currently recognizes nine subspecies of *Boa constrictor* with two in question as to whether or not they are full species (*orophias* and *nebulosus*). Most of these subspecies, with the exception of a few, are poorly differentiated from each other (taxonomically). The papers and original descriptions that were written are very vague and the descriptions are short and not very informative. Some descriptions were written and published based on a single specimen from a particular location. However, we must respect these descriptions for what they are worth and work with them to try and identify what we see today as *Boa constrictor*s. Interpretation is the key.

It's not as easy as it sounds because of the nature of some boas being similar to some degree to their neighbors. For example certain *Boa c. constrictor* from the Amazon Basin are quite similar from country to country. But, there are subtle differences that a trained eye can detect. For the longest time I have heard hobbyists say that there is no way of identifying whether a boa is from Guyana or Suriname. However, after many years of seeing shipments of both, I can see some very obvious differences and a few subtle ones.

It's the same with the Central American *Boa c. imperator.* Most localities have certain distinguishable attributes for each country from which they come. However, all of them have scale counts that fit within the parameters of *Boa c imperator* (even the subspecies *Boa c. sabogae).* Therefore we must look to their morphological differences. All of these things are reasons why the old descriptions are too vague and that it is just recently that we can get exact locality data on animals and compare them to what is already known to science.

I don't claim to be a taxonomist and I don't want to redefine boa taxonomy. However, I do want to elaborate as much as possible on each subspecies and their neighbors and compile as much written information and experience that I can to help better identify each one of these subspecies. I also want to emphasize the fact that by simply observing these creatures in captivity, viewing their breeding habits and feeding habits, we can get a better idea about what makes each one of these localities of boas different from each other.

Evolution

Let's start from the beginning in Gondwanaland, the ancient former super continent in the Southern Hemisphere, which included South America, Africa, peninsular India, Australia, and Antarctica. The name was coined by the Austrian geologist Eduard Suess in reference to the Upper Paleozoic and Mesozoic formations of the Gondwana region of central India, which display typical developments of some of the shared geologic features.

The concept that the continents were at one time joined in the geologic past was first set forth in detail by Alfred Wegener, a German meteorologist, in 1915. He envisioned a single great landmass, Pangaea, which supposedly began to separate late in the Triassic Period (245 to 208 million years ago). Wegener's hypothesis of continental drift was based on the apparent geographic "fit" of the bulge of eastern South America and the western coast of Africa. Although the term "Gondwanaland" does not appear in the modern literature with great frequency, the concept of continental drift and former continental connections is widely accepted in the scientific community today.

So what does Gondwanaland have to do with *Boa constrictor*? If we look to Gondwanaland we see that there really was no Central America at that time as it may have been submerged under the ocean. This leads us to believe that the species *Boa constrictor* started in South America and that all the subspecies that we know of today evolved from the South American *Boa constrictor*. Some boas headed north into what is now Central America and its islands as it formed and these boas evolved based on environmental and climatic influences. Others headed south into cooler highlands or west through valleys in the Andes mountains (that very well may be snow-capped mountains today), into deserts, or east into rainforests. Whatever the case, through genetic isolation, evolution has changed these animals - and some into significantly different creatures compared to their neighboring subspecies which may not be very far away. I feel that the answers would be found in fossil records of which there are none discovered so far. Therefore we are back to where we started and thus the main reason for the confusion of this taxon.

Carolus Linnaeus

Taxonomy is the classification of all living organisms based on their evolutionary relationships to each other. The first taxonomist to successfully catalog living things was Carolus Linnaeus in the mid 1700s and his method is still in use today. Linnaeus devised a hierarchical system of classification in which all life is classified into a series of categories or taxa. These taxa exist in descending order from most inclusive to least inclusive and pertaining to *Boa constrictor* are as follows:

Kingdom: Animalia
Phylum: Chordata
Class: Reptilia
Order: Squamata
Family: Boidae
Genus: ***Boa***
Species: *constrictor*
Subspecies: All subspecies of *Boa constrictor*

Carolus Linnaeus was known as the Father of Taxonomy. He was responsible for describing the genus and species of *Boa constrictor* in 1758 in his pamphlet called *Systema Naturae*. Linnaeus updated his *Systema Naturae* constantly, which grew from a slim pamphlet to a multi volume work with a 13th edition that comprised 3,000 pages in 1770. As he updated, he described thousands of new species of plants and animals that were brought to him from exotic places. However, Linnaeus did not travel to these places and therefore had no experience with the living animals and their habitat.

In his early years, Linnaeus believed that the *Species* was not only real, but unchangeable - as he wrote, *Unitas in omni specie ordinem ducit* (The invariability of species is the condition for order in nature.) But Linnaeus contradicted this when he observed how different species of plants and animals might hybridize, to create forms which looked like new species. He abandoned the concept that species were fixed and invariable, and suggested that some - perhaps most - species in a genus might have arisen through hybridization. Linnaeus also theorized that plant and animal species might be altered through the process of acclimatization. All of his evolutionary beliefs totally pertain to *Boa constrictor* as we see it today within its diverse natural habitat of genetically isolated islands, deserts, rainforests, and cloud forests. These boas may in fact have all shared a common ancestor and over time were genetically isolated from each other. Then as time passed (tens of thousands of years) two or more groups may have become genetically connected either by rising or lowering of sea level or rising or lowering of mountains. Therefore interbreeding or hybridization occurs and a new species or subspecies is born. This is all just theory, but it makes a lot of sense, especially when you look at the similarities of boas and their neighboring subspecies.

Towards the end of his life, Linnaeus investigated what he thought were cases of crosses between plant genera, and suggested that, perhaps, new genera might also arise through hybridization. I also found it ironic to learn that Linnaeus wrote *"Creationis telluris est gloria Dei ex opere Naturae per Hominem solum"* ("The Earth's creation is the glory of God, as seen from the works of Nature by Man alone") in a later edition of *Systema Naturae*.

Charles Darwin

Charles Darwin was the British naturalist who became famous for his theories of evolution and natural selection. His most significant accomplishment may have been his five week stay in the Galapagos Islands back in 1835. It was here that he studied the incredible diversity of plants, reptiles, mammals and birds of this small archipelago in the Pacific Ocean. It was also here that Darwin started to believe that all the life on Earth evolved over millions of years from a few common ancestors. His ideas were that evolution is induced by mutations and natural selection and that these mutations favor genetic variety. However, natural selection on the contrary, limits the genetic variety and evolution is therefore continuous and not a number of species following one another. Speciation then occurs when a genetic pool is divided in two or more isolated parts. This occurs when two populations become reproductively isolated from each other (genetic isolation - in Darwin's case - an island in an Archipelago). When this happens, the organism and its environment change and each become a unique species. Therefore, Darwin's theory of evolutionary selection holds that variation within species occurs randomly and that the survival or extinction of each organism is determined by that organism's ability to adapt to its environment. Darwin also keyed the phrase "Survival of the Fittest".

I mention Darwin in this chapter because I believe that his ideas of evolution also fully pertain to what we see in *Boa constrictor* today.

Lothar Forcart

I thought it was necessary to mention Lothar Forcart as he was the taxonomist responsible for the re-classification of *Boa constrictor* that we use today.

While revising the family *Boidae* at the Museum of Natural History in Basle, Switzerland (1951), Lothar Forcart observed some names in Olive Griffith Stull's "A Check list of the family *Boidae"(1935)*. Stull accepted the designation by Stejneger of *Boa canina* (Linnaues 1758) as a type species of *Boa (Boa canina* at the time was what is now considered Tree Boas or *Corallus caninus)*. Stejneger based this designation on a process of elimination. The process of elimination is NOT accepted by the International Rules on Zoological Nomenclature and therefore the genus *Boa* with *Boa canina* as a type species was dropped and *Corallus* (described by Daudin 1803) was used to replace it.

So now we come to where the real genus *Boa* comes into the picture. The genus was already accepted but as you can see it was juggled between *Corallus* and *Boa.* Also, since there was confusion between the two names, Laurenti (1768) changed the genus name *Boa* to *Constrictor* in a paper Titled "Synopsin Reptilium". So Forcart looked back in time to the type selection by Fitzinger (1843) who designated *Boa constrictor* as the genotype of *Boa.* This was then validated and therefore accepted by the scientific community as the full genus and was also backed by the fact that Linnaeus had already used *Boa* as a genus name in 1758. At the same time *Constrictor* was considered a genus also (Laurenti 1768) and this too was then synonimized with *Boa.* Consequently the end result was that *Constrictor* (Laurenti) became a synonym of *Boa* (Linnaues). Lothar Forcart then re-listed the following species and subspecies of the genus *Boas*: *Boa constrictor constrictor, Boa constrictor amarali, Boa constrictor imperator, Boa constrictor ocidentalis, Boa constrictor sabogae, Boa constrictor sigma* and *Boa orophias.*

Selective Breeding in Captivity

A lot of boa enthusiasts and breeders do not realize the impact of selective breeding on captive populations of boas. In captivity we can leap ahead hundreds (if not thousands) of years in "evolution". We can do this simply by selectively breeding for certain traits. Take for example the Hog Island Boa. The first Hog Island Boas I saw that came out of the wild in the mid-Eighties were dark brown with a lot of black speckling. But, through selective breeding we see an almost speckle-less boa today. This was done in just two or three generations of selectively breeding boas to each other that had less and less speckles. A similar scenario could take thousands of years to occur in nature. This then also brings up the topic of un-natural selection where in 50 years the boas in captivity could look completely different from what their cousins in nature looked like. Another question would be "Could these boas then be reintroduced into their native habitat and could they survive without the cryptic patterns and colors they once displayed?"

All of this information that I have read and observed brings me to the conclusion that although most of the *Boa constrictor* subspecies may look similar, there are very distinguishable differences. These differences are all based on the fact that they all are somewhat genetically isolated from each other and rarely interbreed in nature. The problem occurs or questions arise as to the validity of these supposed subspecies when crossbreeding occurs in captivity. However, we cannot go by these incidences as far more genetically different creatures have been cross bred in captivity (Zebras X Donkeys = Zonkeys, Lions X Tigers = Ligers and Burmese Pythons X Reticulated Pythons = Borneo Bat-eating Pythons).

Chapter TWO: Boa Constrictors as Pets

Boa constrictors are ranked among the top five reptilian pets in the industry. Thousands are sold each year in the U.S. from private breeders and 10's of thousands are sold to pets shops from wholesalers that get them as farmed imports. Boas are quite popular for a few reasons. They do not get very large compared to the giant pythons which easily reach 10 feet in a relatively short period of time.

An average sized adult boa from Colombia may reach 7 feet. There are always exaggerated stories about a giant boa that is over 10 feet. I personally have measured hundreds of large Boas and not one that I have seen has come even close to 10 feet. The average size of a Central American boa is barely 5 feet and some of the island form boas mature at just less than 5 feet in length. Boa constrictors are also quite handleable and calm snakes and pose no threat to their adult human handlers.

Boas make wonderful pets for the entire family. John Mack and his mom, Amy show off their motley Argentine Boa from Reptiles by Mack. Children should be supervised with these and any reptile pets. Photo by Bob Ashley.

To date there are no documented cases of a human being severely injured or killed by a boa. Even though they are quite tame it is always recommended that children be supervised when handling any type of boa – big or small. Boas require little care as far as feeding, watering and housing and could be left unfed for weeks with no harm whatsoever to the snake's health as long as an ample water supply and heat is available. Boas are also long-lived and to purchase one may be a 20 + year commitment. I personally have had a few boas in my collection for over 15 years. And finally – with the plethora of colors, type localities, pattern anomalies and various sizes, it is no wonder why the demand is so high for these beautiful and ornate creatures.

WHERE TO FIND A BOA

Pet & Specialty Stores

Many pet stores offer boas for sale. Not only are they offering boas for pets, but they are exhibiting healthy animals in proper and inspiring set-ups. Many are offering correct advice and stocking the best equipment and supplies for their customers. In the past, pet stores rarely established proper enclosures to keep snakes long-term. Heating and diet were inappropriate and specimens were often in poor health and occasionally species were mixed together in a single cage. As imported specimens made up most of the boas for sale in the shops, most were traumatized and parasitized. Now, however, most stores are offering captive-born or farm-raised boas and they are installing larger enclosures with heat, water, and a healthy diet. Many are even offering veterinary services to care for boas before or during sales times.

Shows and Expos

In recent years, reptile shows and expos have become very popular. In the last few years there has been an increase in the number of captive-produced boas at these shows. Typically the specimens offered at these shows are healthy, feeding well, and excellent specimens to begin a snake-keeping hobby or to add to an existing collection. At these shows you get the rare opportunity to hand pick the snake you want to purchase. When having a snake shipped to you, there is always the risk of receiving a snake that is picked by someone who may not have your best interest at heart. Add to the savings of not having to pay shipping and the lack of stress placed on the animal from shipping and the shows and expos are often an excellent opportunity to get a really nice boa.

The top U.S. shows include the National Reptile Breeders Expo in Florida, the N.A.R.B.C. shows in Anaheim, Chicago and Arlington, and the ETHS Conference and Expo in Houston. There are dozens of other great local shows throughout the country. These shows can be located on the internet, through local herpetological societies, and they are advertised in reptile magazines and journals. It is well worth the effort to track them down.

Cage Requirements

Boas are ectothermic or cold-blooded creatures that need to thermoregulate their body temperature by moving towards heat to digest food when necessary and by getting away from the heat and hide when needed. Therefore these heating requirements must be met in order to keep your pet boa alive and thriving in your captive conditions. You must first understand what type of climatic conditions your particular boa requires (tropical rainforest or semi arid) then create a mini micro climate for that snake. Sudden changes in temperature in your home may cause stress to your boa so the caging you buy or make must be able to hold the micro climate conditions in spite of what happens in your home in terms of temperature and humidity. Even though certain temperature dropping and humidity loss may be advantageous to manipulate breeding, these conditions may be very stressful for a pet boa that is not in breeding condition and used to consistent temperatures and feeding regimens.

TYPES OF CAGING

There are many different types of commercially built boa cages available in the pet trade today. Again I must emphasize the fact that you should get one that will accommodate your needs as far as temperatures and humidity. The cage should also be escape-proof and if not, certain changes must be made to keep it secured at all times.

Glass Aquariums

Although glass aquariums are commonly used and sold in pet shops and they are aesthetically pleasing, I do not recommend using them for your boa. Many pet shops stock them for use with reptiles and these glass structures make for a good home for a desert lizard or hamster. But the screen top is not conducive to proper Boa constrictor care. These tops do not help keep humidity in and therefore your boa will get very dry and in a very short period of time. The screens also act like a cheese grater on the boa's nose and some may constantly scrape their noses to the point of severe damage that may require veterinary care. At one time in the past the only option was to use aquariums as enclosures for pet snakes. However, today there are a plethora of commercially built enclosures for pet boas that are far superior to glass aquarium.

Wood or Melamine Caging

Cages made of wood work well for housing boas. Some cabinet makers make excellent boa cages that are both aesthetically pleasing and conducive to proper boa care. Wooden cages however need to be properly "Wood Sealed" and their finish should be completely dry before putting your pet in them. It's not worth your time to build a cage and not seal it properly as fecal material and moisture will warp the structure and cleaning / disinfecting the enclosure will be next to impossible. In my opinion I find homemade wooden cages hard to heat properly and they tend to be mite magnets with all their nooks and crannies for mites to hide and reproduce. They are also VERY heavy and hard to move. It may not be worth the time and cost of wood and glass to build a cage when you can buy a commercially built plastic one for the same amount of money or less. But if you do use wooden structures, you can use the same guidelines below for heating and sizing.

Plastic Boa Cages

Plastic caging has become quite popular in the past 10 years and they make excellent enclosures for boas. They are easy to clean, light weight, mites cannot find too many places to hide in them, they keep their shape under humid conditions, are stackable, and they are affordably priced.

PVC enclosures make excellent homes for captive boas. Photo by Kevin McCurley.

I maintain larger mainland form adult boas in 5 and 6 foot long enclosures. These plastic enclosures are 24-36 inches deep and 14 - 18 inches high.

I maintain dwarf or island race boas in 3-4 foot long cages that are 24 inches deep and 18 inches high.

The cages are fitted with a 12 inch by 24 inch heat pad underneath the unit that is connected to a thermostat and set to the proper temperature. The heat pad is placed to one side of the enclosure and runs front to back. If you need more basking heat, many of these plastic enclosures have a recessed area to fit a heat lamp in them. Again you must try different watt light bulbs to figure out the ideal "Hot Spot" for your boa.

Healthy boas will thrive in captivity if they can thermoregulate their body temperature. Therefore the proper size cage is important. A larger sized boa may have trouble avoiding the hot spots in a small enclosure because they are so large and can not get away from the heat. The same problem can occur if a small boa is put into a very large enclosure and it has a hard time finding the hot spot. A good general rule of thumb would be to have a boa housed in a one foot to one foot ratio (a 4 foot long boa would be very happy in a 4 foot long enclosure).

This living room setup of PVC cages from Zoo Products is not only beautiful but also functional for keeping and breeding a number of boas and pythons. Photo by Kevin McCurley.

Rack Systems

Rack systems work very well when raising large groups of youngsters, subadults, or even dwarf adults. They are stackable and could house many animals in a small space. Many are made commercially out of plastic and use Iris®, Rubbermaid®, or Sterilite® plastic storage containers as enclosures for your snakes. These structures are used like a drawer system in that the storage bins simply slide into the rack and the supports from top and bottom create a lidless system. They are usually heated from beneath each level in the rack with the heat tape towards the back of the rack or are heated from behind with heat tape. The heat tape is then connected to a thermostat and adjusted accordingly. The storage bins used in the rack systems come in many sizes from shoe box size for newborns (12" x 6") to blanket size for adults (37" X 17"). I have even maintained some of my mature dwarf Nicaraguan and island boas in CB70 Iris® trays (37" X 17") and they thrive and even breed in these racks with plenty of room. I highly recommend rack system for boas as they are easily heated, hold proper humidity, and small boas can thermoregu-

Rack systems are ideal for keeping a number of snakes in a small space.

late properly in them and they are readily available from commercial dealers and are aesthetically pleasing too.

Many commercial boa breeders today use both Freedom Breeder® rack systems and the new Vision® rack systems. Both use Iris® storage containers and are available in a few different sizes. Both are lidless systems. The Freedom Breeder® rack uses a screened top while the Vision® system uses a top that is a molded plastic with multiple configurations of holes.

I like the Vision® plastic top because you can choose more or less holes to match up the humidity requirements for your particular race of boa.

Detail of one of the drawers in the rack system seen above.

Boas

Heating

The temperatures mentioned here will be for Non-Breeding Boas that are maintained as pets. More about temperature manipulation will be covered in the chapter on Breeding.

As mentioned earlier Boa constrictors are ectothermic and require a hot spot to regulate their body temperature. Most boas thrive in captive conditions with an ambient temperature in their enclosure of 80 – 85º F in the day and can tolerate a few degrees drop at night. A hot spot of 88 – 95º F is recommended for boas and this can be created in a few different ways. Heat tape commercially made in 3 to 12 inch widths and can be cut to any length (comes in rolls of 50 feet) can be adhered outside and under a plastic enclosure (as not to harm the snake in case it may ever get too hot).

There is a wide range of heating products available to keepers.

Heat pads are also commercially made that have adhesive and stick directly under your enclosure. It obviously would be tough to heat a wooden unit in this manner as heat tape relies on heat transfer, however this method will create a nice hot spot in a plastic cage.

I use aluminum foil tape that is used for duct work to adhere the 3 – 12 inch heat tape as it adheres to almost anything and lasts a very long time. I recommend the heat tape be placed to one side of the enclosure to take up approximately one quarter of the floor space. In a larger cages you can put two lengths of heat tape (side by side) on the back of the cage. This configuration creates a warm side and a cooler side. Thus thermoregulation is easily accomplished because your boa will be able to choose its desired temperature. Some keepers use light bulbs for heat as they create a very direct heat spot that the snake can bask under. Light bulbs will work far better than heat tape in a wooden or melamine cage. But household spot lights will create a very hot spot that is directed into a small area. This could cause severe burns on your boas. Therefore I recommend a spot light made specifically for reptile enclosures. Some keepers use both light bulbs and heat tape and simply adjust their wattage and thermostats accordingly. They then keep the light on a timer set to a 12 hours on / 12 hours off and leave the heat tape on 24 hours a day to keep the ambient temperature up during cooler weather.

Either way – both sources of heat work well, however, light bulbs tend to dry out your enclosure which is not a healthy environment for a Boa. Some breeders in the more southern parts of the U.S. use space heaters for the entire room. I do not recommend this as it does not help in proper digestion as the boas will not have a hot spot but rather a hot room.

WARNING - Space heaters and improperly installed heat tape can create a fire hazard.

Temperature Control

Now that you have your "Heaters" in place you need to regulate how much heat you want them to emit. I highly recommend a commercially made reptile thermostat as there are many on the market to choose from. These thermostats come fully equipped with a temperature probe that is placed in the desired position directly above or below your heat source to "taste" the air

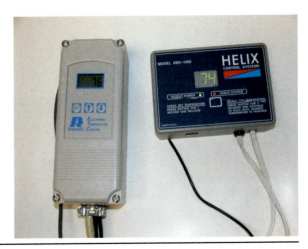

and tell the thermostat to kick on or turn off. The more expensive thermostats never really turn off but rather they power down when it gets hot and power up when temps drop. I set my thermostats to 92° F in the summer when my boas are feeding regularly and turn them down slightly in the winter to around 87° F.

Thermostats come in different models that can handle from 100 watts to 1000 watts and light bulbs are individually rated in watts. Heat tape is 10 watts per foot for the 3 inch and 20 watts per foot for the 12 inch. So check how many watts you have before buying your thermostat.

Heat Tape & Pads

Heat tape is made in 3", 4" and 11" width and is cut to length. This product is designed to be operated at a "herp-related" temperature and is an excellent heating material for herpetoculturists. The product is commercially available and is sold as Flexwatt® heat tape. It is ultra-thin, at .012 inches thick, and is sealed in flexible polyurethane. This product is a "Do It Yourself" project and you will need to supply the wire and plug. The heat tape is connected to two clips and two clip covers which are wired to standard electrical wire. You must use a rheostat or a proportional thermostat with this product as it will get very hot if not manipulated.

WARNING! Because this is a product that you manipulate yourself, there is no implied warranty and you incur all liability for it. Keep tape under 95° F with the use of a thermostat.

Heat Panels

Heat panels are another type of heating element that works well for boas. They are suspended from the ceiling of the enclosure and radiate the heat they make downward. These too work in a similar manner to the ceramic heating elements; however, they do not get as hot and have a more even heat (instead of pointing in one very hot spot). Heat panels should be connected to a thermostat to ensure proper temperature gradient. And lastly, they could dry out your enclosure if humidity is not kept in check.

Infrared Ceramic Heating Elements

This product was originally used in Europe to speed up the process of drying enamel paints. These heating elements look like a light bulb and screw into a light bulb socket. However, they give off NO light and are all ceramic. As for use with Boas – this product does work well in heating your Boa's enclosure. But they definitely should be used in conjunction with a thermostat as they get very HOT. As a matter of fact they may get too hot. This product must be kept far away from you and your pet. You must never come in contact with this product as severe burns can occur.

Note: I do not recommend using ceramic heating elements because they tend to dry out your Boa enclosure very quickly and if unchecked could create unsafe conditions for you and your boa.

Humidity

Humidity is the amount of water vapor in the air. In the case of keeping boas it is the amount of water vapor (humidity) in the air of

Humidity is important for the well-being of boas, especially during the shedding process. Photo by Nathan Hanks.

your Boa's enclosure. It's well known that warmer air will hold more humidity than cooler air. Therefore in order to keep the proper humidity levels for your boa, you must have HEAT. Humidity can be accomplished in a few different ways. You can manually spray your boas and their substrate on a daily basis with a hand held pump sprayer or mister. I prefer this method because it keeps me in closer touch with my boas and their health. This method also works well because you can give the boas more water vapor when needed and less to those that do not require as much. You can also leave a tub or basin of water (large enough for your boa to climb into and soak) inside your boa enclosure. This basin can be filled when needed and should be placed on the opposite end from the heat or hot spot. Another method to increase humidity is by placing a basin filled with moistened sphagnum moss in your enclosure. All of these methods work well, however, a keeper should remember that keeping your boa too wet can be just as harmful as keeping them too dry. Constant warm, wet and stagnant air conditions can lead to mold in your enclosure and even worse, skin fungus on your boa. Although most boas thrive in a high humidity environment, when in the wild they are in the open air of the rainforest and do not get exposed to such stagnant conditions as in a captive environment. Therefore air circulation is the key in maintaining proper humidity levels in your boa's cage. All Boa enclosures should have proper screened ventilation holes that can be either covered to increase humidity or opened to decrease humidity. I must also emphasize that the humidity in your boas enclosure will always be much higher in summer as compared to winter conditions in your home. My boas are happy with a humidity level of around 80% in summer and a winter humidity of around 50 – 60%. Boas do not mind a slight drop in humidity in the winter – especially with a little bit more of a drop in temperature at night. I must bring this up because in the past it was assumed that boas needed to be wet and rained on in the winter, when in fact, wild boas see far less rain during their winter months (dry season) and far more rain during the summer or rainy seasons. Therefore these conditions should be duplicated in captivity.

Substrate

There are many kinds of commercially made reptile cage substrates on the market today. It will all depend on the environment in your

Cypress mulch (left) and shredded aspen (right) are excellent substrates for boas.

home as to which one will work best for you. Some homes with hot forced air heating will dry out the home environment very quickly.

Therefore you would need a substrate that holds more moisture. I prefer cypress mulch as it is easy to get in pet shops or home improvement centers. It comes in many sized bags and is usually already moist in its packaging. It does not rot, resists mold, and holds a lot of moisture while keeping its top surface dry. It can be rehydrated if it dries out by simply spraying it with water. This product looks nice and very much resembles a jungle floor, therefore making your boa more at home.

Please note that you should be very careful at feeding time and make sure that your boas do not ingest large pieces of cypress mulch. The commercial "double shredded" variety is highly recommended as it has no large pieces in it that could get caught in your boa's mouth or digestive tract.

Another substrate that works well in homes with a little more humidity is shredded aspen bedding. This product is also easy to get in a pet shop and comes in large bales too. It is a dry substrate but can be sprayed lightly (do not soak it as it may get moldy). It smells very nice and looks aesthetically pleasing too.

And lastly, the good old standby – *Newspaper.* I use newspaper on all of my boas (adults and newborns) simply because it holds moisture and is quick and easy to change. I can get it in an endless supply for no money and its soy bean based ink is clean and completely harmless to boas.

Drinking Water

Water is very important to your boa's health. For adult boas I prefer to keep a large tub (big enough for the boa to climb into) inside the boas' enclosures. I keep this tub on the cool side of my boa's unit for the whole summer and change the water every other day or as soon as they defecate in it. I also use a large dog bowl style water dish and keep this filled with water and change that every other day. I use

bleach to disinfect the water tubs and bowls at least once a week. I can't emphasize enough the fact that your boas have to have fresh clean water available at all times. In the winter I remove the tubs and just use the large bowls for water. If your boa constantly tips the water basin, then add bricks or rocks in it to keep it more stable.

For baby boas I use small 8 ounce plastic deli cups for water and change their water every other day. I do not clean these cups as they are very inexpensive and I simply throw out the soiled cup and replace it with new. I also like to use a ceramic 4 inch water crock and I place the 8 ounce cup in the crock as it acts as a liner and therefore I don't have to clean the crock. The crock also keeps the youngsters from tipping it over as it is quite heavy.

Note: I do not recommend a large water bowl for wild-caught boas as they may seek this area for security and defecate in it. If they set in this foul water they could contract disease as bacteria grows quickly in this environment. I also do not recommend a large water bowl if you cannot be disciplined enough to change the water on daily basis.

Hide Boxes & Shelves

A hide box should be available to your boa at all times. I prefer to have two hide boxes (especially for a new acquisition or wild-caught boa). I put one hide on the cooler side of the enclosure and one on the warmer side. This way the boa can choose its most comfortable place in the enclosure to feel secure. Anything can be used as a hide box as long as it  is not thin plywood, pressboard, or cardboard (they will rot under high humidity conditions). A cat litter pan turned upside down with a hole in the top works well. A few commercially produced plastic hide boxes are available also. I also use cork bark rolls as they make excellent hiding places for boas. They can be used as a tube or cut in half to make a half pipe style that can be placed with the concave side down. The hiding place should be the same size as the snake in its coiled position or smaller as boas like to squeeze into tight spaces. A hide box can also be used as a humidity chamber if you live in a dry environment. The bottom of the box can simply be partially filled with sphagnum moss and moistened to the snake's liking.

Shelves within your boa enclosure work well and add floor space to your cage. You can add almost two thirds more floor space by adding a shelf. Boas also like to pick their ideal temperature to thermoregulate, therefore the more places they can choose from, the better. Boas also tend to stalk food items from a hanging position. A shelf could simulate a large branch from which a boa can hang its head to ambush prey.

Lighting

Boa constrictors do not require any special care when it comes to lighting and could thrive in captive conditions with very little light. However, although full-spectrum lighting is not necessary for proper boa care, I still recommend using it as these full-spectrum bulbs bring out the magnificent colors of your boa and help you view your pets more easily. Most commercially built vivariums have a place for a full-spectrum fluorescent light fixture or a place for an incandescent light fixture.

These lighting fixtures should be connected to a timer to create a 12 hour on / 12 hour off light cycle. Boas need this light cycle for proper care and it is highly recommended to be very disciplined at keeping the cycle going for your boa. Even though you want your boa to be exposed to good light, they also require a very dark night time.

If you live in the northern parts of the world and

Boas will bask under a warm bulb. Also, full-spectrum bulbs will bring out the magnificent colors of your boa and help you view your pets more easily. Photo by Nathan Hanks.

have very short winter days, your boas may notice these short days (even though their over head lighting is on) and may go off food. This is not a problem and you may want to shorten the daylight hours to 10 and 14 hours of night. Whether you have a single pet or a room full of boas it is imperative that your animals have a proper light cycle. In a commercial breeding environment I recommend that you use 6-8 foot long fluorescent fixtures in the ceiling of your boa room. This will save money and electricity when compared to lighting each and every boa enclosure. These fixtures can be wired to a commercial timer that also acts as an on/off switch in manual mode. Lighting the whole room with a good full-spectrum bulb is not only aesthetically pleasing but conducive of proper boa care when it comes to being able to see full clear view of all the boas in their cages.

A dark unlit boa cage can lead to a mite infestation in a very short time. Also, in a dark enclosure you can overlook a poor shedding cycle which could lead to a skin infection. I cannot emphasize enough the fact that you need good lighting in your boa room or enclosure.

Cleanup & Maintenance

I clean my hands with anti-bacterial soap before and after handling and cleaning my boas. I also use rubber gloves when cleaning enclosures and I clean out my boas' enclosures weekly. Every morning I look for defecation and I will spot clean as I see them occur. Since boas in captive conditions tend to lay on their substrate constantly, it is recommended to change that substrate very often. Boas can get sores or bacterial infections under their skin if left in direct contact with urine for even a brief period of time. The bare cages should also be cleaned with a disinfectant and or bleach to rid them of any germs, bacteria and odors left behind from your boa's defecation. Scouring pads soaked in bleach or antibacterial soap works well for getting out those stains left from hardened urates. I also use the scouring pads to clean the walls of the enclosure as boas can get quite messy at feeding time and defecation.

Water bowls should also be cleaned regularly with bleach and water as to keep bacteria down as it grows quite quickly in warm wet conditions. If a water bowl is defecated in it should also be cleaned immedi-

L-R: Bleach, Alphazyme Plus, Nolvasan, glass cleaner, citrus-based de-greaser.

ately with bleach. You should keep your boa as clean as possible and as sterile as possible – especially if you own more than one boa. Even though a true sterile environment is next to impossible to duplicate – it is only done to help prevent spread of any disease or ectoparasites (mites) and is also done for the health of your boa can be better maintained under clean conditions.

Chapter THREE: Feeding

Boa constrictor feeding on a thawed rat.

*Boa constrictor*s in the wild are opportunistic feeders and will feed on many forms of prey items. *Boa c. imperator* is known to eat large Ctenosaurs (Spiny-tailed iguanas) and Green Iguanas in the wild. Some large adult boas may eat birds, agoutis, rodents, rabbits and squirrels. Baby boas in the wild may prey on geckos and tree frogs. However, in captivity it is best to maintain *Boa constrictor*s on rodents and rabbits. Both are easy to purchase at a local pet shop as live food or as frozen food items. In the past most of the rodents sold to the pet trade were surplus from laboratories that breed them to sell for research. However, today there are many commercial rodent facilities that breed these rodents specifically as food for reptiles. This has also become big business in the U.S. with hundreds of thousands of frozen rodents sold monthly.

A lot of boa breeders and hobbyists also breed their own rodents to feed their boas. This has become quite common with serious breeders and sometimes maintaining the rodents may take up as much time as maintaining the boas. Buying frozen rodents can be quite costly as compared to raising your own. However, raising rodents is no easy task never mind the smell. Therefore the choice is up to the enthusiast as to whether or not they have the time to maintain a breeding colony of rodents or to simply buy them frozen. Most adult boas will accept a defrosted rodent just as quickly as a live one. But there are some scenarios with younger boas that will have a tendency to only want live food items or fresh, humanely killed food items. In that case you may want to just raise one small group of rodents for those finicky feeders.

The number one mistake most novices make in raising their boas is "Over Feeding". Boas evolved to sustain themselves on a minimal amount of food. Therefore you don't want to over feed or even starve your boas, but rather maintain a healthy weight. A young boa can thrive on a single meal that leaves a slight lump once every 10 to 14 days. At this regimen they will have a slower but steadier growth rate and could maintain themselves until adulthood.

It is also best to create a more seasonal type of environment for adult boas (which will happen automatically in your home because of the seasons that are going on outside your home). Mature Boas will detect these season, whether it be a near by window that they are exposed to natural light cycles or simply the few degree difference in temperatures from season to season. Your boas will detect these changes and may even refuse food. This is a good thing because you really do not want your boa to feed all year round as it is not natural. Adult boas should be fed a meal that leaves a mild-sized lump once every two to three weeks. Although Boas are very capable of eating very large food items, I tend to avoid these scenarios as it is not healthy for your boas to eat this way.

Feeding Neonate & Sub Adult Boas

Baby boas may require the movement of a live prey item in order to initiate a strike. Therefore the first meals of your baby boa may need to be live hopper mice or baby rats. After a few meals in this manner most boas will easily accept a defrosted mouse from forceps. Frozen mice or rat pups can be defrosted by simply leaving them out in your herp room overnight to be ready for feeding by morning. Or if you can't wait you can soak the food items in warm

Baby *Boa constrictor* feeding on a hopper mouse.

water until they are fully thawed. I sometimes change the water a few times to keep the food item warm. This way when you dry it off to feed to your pet it will still be warm and the boa senses the heat coming from the prey item. This will elicit a quicker feeding response. Baby boas that are to be considered shoulder pets should eat an appropriately sized meal every week to 10 days. The meal should leave a slight lump in the boas body and should not be so noticeable that it spreads the scales of the snake. You should switch to defrosted prey items as soon as possible because live rodents could possibly injure your boa. Young hopper mice will probably not injure a baby boa. However, larger mice and rats could easily hurt or even kill a boa that may be uninterested in a meal. So never leave a boa unattended with a live prey item.

The size of the prey item should increase with the size of your snake as it grows. However, the schedule of feeding (1 week to 10 days) should be extended as the boa grows. For example, the boa's meal may increase in size – but he may eat only every 10 – 21 days.

Feeding Adult Boas

Adult boas that are not in a breeding program should be fed a meal that will leave a slightly noticeable lump every 14 – 30 days. This is obviously based on a few compensating factors such as heat (Boas that are kept very warm will digest more quickly), size of your boa (large boas can eat one large meal but it may be monthly), and seasons (Adult boas may refuse meals in the winter). Adult boas will thrive in captivity on a diet of just rats. They could easily sustain an entire lifetime on rats. I like to feed larger boas small rabbits (2-3 pounds) as they have less fat than rats. A large boa can sustain itself on one rabbit per month for its entire life.

Defrosted prey items are also preferred as they are much easier to store and will not harm your boa. Again, food items can be defrosted by leaving out over night or soaking in warm water and then drying them off. You must also use judgment when feeding adult boas. If your boa is constantly looking for food and may even strike at the glass when you walk by, you must either feed it a larger item per feeding or feed it more often. But boas that can thermoregulate properly will feed, thermoregulate, and defecate in a very predictable manner. And lastly, if your boa is constantly hungry and you do not plan on breeding it you should try and turn the heat down a bit. Female boas may feed ravenously in late summer and fall if they are sexually mature. Most breeders take this time to "Pump Up" their females for the breeding season ahead. However, if you do not want to breed your boa I recommend keeping it a bit cooler than usual and feed less often.

Shedding

Boas shed throughout their entire lives. Baby boas have their first shed a week to 10 days after birth. After that first shed they will shed according to how much they grow. This directly corresponds with how much they are fed. If fed every week to 10 days they may shed every 4-6 weeks. But as they mature and growth slows down they may only shed every 8 weeks or so.

Mature adults may only shed but a few times a year. The onset of shedding starts with the boas eyes becoming opaque or blue. This is

Retained eye cap.

because boas will shed their eye caps along with the skin. The opaque or blue condition of the eyes is the process of the eye cap separating from the new cap beneath. The same goes for the skin on the entire body as it too looks opaque and faded at first as it starts the process of separating old from new skin. The whole process could take a week to ten days and can be sped up with increased heat or slowed down with lower temperatures. The boa's eyes and skin will clear up towards the end of the cycle and look normal – then starting from the

Stuck shed.

Boas

nose will push and peel the skin and shed from head to tail. The shed skin should come off all in one piece and will look like a rolled up sock.

Some boas will have a problem shedding the old skin if kept too dry. Boas that cannot shed their skin because of dry conditions should be soaked in a tub of shallow warm water for a few hours and then manually shed. This is quite easy to do and may require a helping hand. Also, if the boa is very dry it may require an overnight soak in shallow water (no deeper than the highest point of the snake's body.)

Boas usually will not accept food during these shedding cycles and it is recommended that you do not offer them any food or handle them at this time.

Note: Adult boas that are ill or injured may shed very often (once a month). This back to back shedding is a clear sign of illness and should not be overlooked.

Record Keeping

Record Keeping is probably one of the most important disciplines in boa keeping and breeding. I learned many years ago the importance of record keeping and this was reinforced by my friend Eugene Bessette. Eugene's success in breeding snakes in mainly attributed to his meticulous record keeping. Record keeping is important not only to you but to the snake too. It tells you if there is a cycle or rhythm in feeding patterns, helps you identify an optimum time for breeding introductions and proper record keeping of shed, breeding, feeding and birth can help identify a pattern for future breeding attempts.

I use Record Keeping cards that were created by Eugene to this day. They are simple yet efficient. The card is a heavy stock 5" X 7" card with spaces for the following information; ID#, Sex, Tray#, Card#, Common name and Scientific name, Date of Birth – Sire & Dam. There are 3 columns for indication of Feeding – Breeding – Shedding and Bowel movements.

These cards are worth their weight in gold – especially over a longer period of time. This is because you can go back to these cards to

| ID# _____ Sex _____ Cage/Tray# _____ Card # _____ |
| Common Name: _____ Date In: _____ Sire: _____ |
| Scientific Name: _____ Date Out/Died: _____ Dam: _____ |

DATE	ACTION	DATE	ACTION	DATE	ACTION

Ophiological Services 13916 S.W. Archer Road, Archer, FL 32618 (352) 495-3075 Fax (352) 495-2952

Data card.

review what was done in the past and what to expect in the future. I keep my cards on the boa's cage in a clear plastic sleeve that is attached to the front. Every single thing that I witness is marked on the card. As I run out of space I simply use another card and indicate the next number in succession on the new card (card #1 – card #2 etc.). As I may have too many cards in a sleeve at some point – I then place my cards in a index file box and list them by year.

Chapter FOUR: Breeding Boa Constrictors

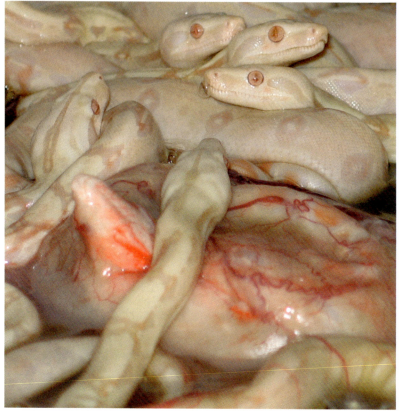

Newborn Albino Boas.

In my opinion there is nothing more gratifying than to having your boas reproduce under your care and maintenance. Breeding *Boa constrictor*s is not as easy as breeding some other popular herps like Corn snakes. But it can be done if the proper conditions are met and sometimes with very good results.

I must emphasize that breeding boas is a great responsibility. Not only to you the keeper - but to the animals themselves. The habit of breeding boas outside their race or locality has been common in the past and most of the time it was due to lack of compatible mates. However, today most keeper and herpetoculturists have much greater knowledge of boas and therefore have an easier time finding acceptable mates. I also would like to emphasize the fact that you are potentially bringing these little creatures into the world and they will need to be placed with other responsible keepers. And lastly, keep in mind that the boas you may be bringing into the world will end up as potential breeders for another keeper one day. Therefore it is important to maintain proper record keeping so that a paper trail of your boa's lineage is available to other keepers in the future.

Sex Determination

Determining sex in boas is not difficult and can be done in two ways. The first way is a method called "Popping". This should only be done with newborn boas as adult boas can be damaged or injured.

Popping is done by gently applying pressure with your thumb and pushing in a rolling manner from a few scales behind the vent towards to the vent. If the boa is a male this gentle pressure should reveal a hemipene. If it's a female there will be nothing there to evert. This method takes a lot of practice and is not 100% as for sex

Popping a young boa . . . In this case, a male.

Popping a young boa . . . In this case, a female.

determination as you could easily mistake a male for female if the hemipenes do not evert. Also – after many years of experience I have noticed that you can put both fingers on the tail (one on top and one on bottom) and roll them gently in a left to right motion. If a hemipene is present you should be able to feel it in the tail. If not – then the baby boa is likely a female.

The best way of determining sex in boas is to probe them. Snake probes are commercially available today and come in a multitude of sizes (the larger the snake the larger the probe and vice versa). The probe should be cleaned with alcohol and dried. Then you should use some kind of lubricant like KY jelly to lubricate the probe. The probe can then be inserted deep into the hemipenes of males or shallow into the cloacas of females. The hemipenes run from the vent towards the tip of the tail. A male boa can probe as many as 25+ subcaudal scales in depth while a female boa may only probe from 3 to 8 subcaudal scales in depth. Some probe depths in male boas that I recorded are as follows; *Boa c. imperator* = 23 and *Boa c. constrictor* = 28.

And lastly, there is another way of determining sex in boas and this is by visually looking at the tails of boas. The tail of an adult male boa will be much longer than that of female. Males also have spurs at the sides of their vents. These vestigial limbs are used to spur

Male Boa 's Spur

Female Boa little to no spur

females during breeding attempts. These spurs are present on female boas, however they are much smaller. The tail of a female boa is much shorter and fatter. Their tails also taper off to a point very quickly compared to the males that have very little taper.

Note: Novice keepers should be very hesitant to pop or probe their own snakes. I highly recommend having an experienced breeder show you the proper techniques.

Breeding Age

All boas reach sexual maturity at different times in their lives. Many compensating factors are involved to determine sexual maturity in boas too. One of these factors is race. Some females of the dwarf races of *Boa c. imperator* may reach sexual maturity at much smaller size of 4-5 feet in length and as young as 3 years in age while larger mainland boas like *Boa c. constrictor* may take as much as 5 or 6 years to mature and should be 6-7 feet in length. Other factors that contribute to sexual maturity are age and muscle mass. A 6 year old boa that may be barely 5 feet in length but has mature muscle mass may breed and produce a beautiful litter while a 2 year old that is barely 5 feet will most likely not reproduce. Males mature sexually much faster than females and breed at a much smaller size. I have had 18 month old males that bred quite well with larger females and yet these young males were only 3.5 feet in length.

Boas that are kept to be used as potential breeders are best kept on a slow and steady diet of rodents. "Slow growing" young boas is a more natural method and helps them mature naturally. They also will gain better muscle mass with slow growing and will develop less fat. You will rarely find a big fat gravid boa in the wild. Most, if not all, are much leaner than most captives I have seen.

If properly fed (and not overfed) most boas should reach sexual maturity in 3-5 years. There are exceptions to this rule but it is definitely not healthy to breed your boas at a very young age as they are most likely too fat and with not enough mature muscle mass. I mention overfeeding because most keepers that feed their boas too much may experience what I call beginner's luck. They obtain a pair of boas and proceed to feed them as much as they will eat. These boas reach a very large size in as little as 18 months and are quickly put into a breeding program. The boas breed successfully and a litter of boas and some (if not all) infertile ova are produced. The breeder then thinks they achieved their goal and tries to "pump up" the female for another breeding trial for the next season. But here is the problem. That female boa that bred at such a young age has lost a significant amount of fat and whatever muscle mass she may have had. Even if she feeds ravenously and gains most of her weight back she will most likely not breed for another year or two or even three. This is because she is in a constant feeding mode and has had no "Feeding – Non-feeding cycle". Yes, this boa produced her first year but only because she was tricked into a "Feeding Cycle" that lasted the first 18 months of her life. She never was exposed to a "Non-feeding Cycle" and if so – it was very short. Therefore this potential breeder was only as good as her first litter.

Feeding Cycles

In the wild boas are exposed to two main seasons. They are a dry season of which it still rains but very little and the rainy season in which it rains almost daily. During the rainy season food is plentiful and boas may have the opportunity to find food and may eat many meals in a short period of time. This should be duplicated in captivity. You can tell when your Boas (especially females) are hungry. It is usually in the warmest wettest time of the year (late Summer and early Fall). Therefore your boas should eat most of their meals for the year in a period of just a few months and then be fed sporadically throughout the rest of the warmer season.

Non Feeding Cycles

In the wild when mature boas are exposed to a dry season and food is hard to find they get a chance to rest and store fat for the seasons ahead. I will never forget when one of my mentors, Eugene Bessette, told me that "Boas grow more when you don't feed them". This spoke volumes to me as Eugene has raised thousands of snakes and has very meticulous feeding records to prove this. Some may ask "How can a boa grow when it is not fed?" That is easy to explain as a boa's metabolism knows when food is in short supply and it starts to store energy. While storing this energy, the boa gains more muscle mass and this is key to getting a female boa into breeding shape. Overfed boas simply pass most if not all of what they eat because they have no time to metabolize it into muscle mass. This is why I feel it is so important to feed boas very sparingly or not at all during their cooler dryer season (late fall and winter).

Temperature Cycling

Along with the rainy and dry seasons, boas experience different temperature exposures. During the wet season boas are subjected to much higher temperatures as hot air carries much more humidity. In captivity this is during our summer when the temperatures are at their warmest and the days are at their longest. Boas are very sensitive to temperature change and light cycles and these indicators tell them to feed or to rest. To induce breeding in boas they must be exposed to the dry season or cooler temperature season. This is done in captivity in the winter and during the shortest days.

Proper daytime ambient winter temperatures for boas should be 78º F with a basking spot of around 84º F. Proper night time ambient temperature should be around 70º F with no supplemental heat or hot spot. The cooler night time temps should coincide with darkness. Since winter days are shorter I like to keep the supplemental heat on during the day from 8 a.m. until 4 p.m. then the heat is turned off and the boas are exposed to the cooler night time temps from 4 p.m. until 8 a.m. when the heat turns back on. This temperature cycle is started by gradually cooling the room over a period two weeks. Then it is maintained for at least 10 weeks. Then it is gradually warmed up over a period of two weeks. The time of year this is done is all based on your geographic location in the world. I would also like to note that I keep all of my boas exposed to these temperature cycles (hatchlings, yearlings, etc.) to get them prepared and dialed into their surroundings.

Introduction

Some breeders introduce males to females at the start of their temperature cycling. Some wait until the coolest months to introduce while others wait until the spring warm up. All of these methods work however, I would recommend introducing the males in the beginning of your temperature cycling. I believe that these initial introductions help the female to start developing follicles. I simply place the male into the female's enclosure for a few days then take him out for a few days. As soon as I see vigorous spurring on the part of the male I leave him in until I see the female ovulating. With boas I also always use a single male to a single female or one-on-one. I rarely try to spread a male thin by breeding him to more than one female as the window of opportunity to fertilize the female is quite short and could easily be missed if the male is off courting another female.

Courting

Male boas are relentless with courting a female and will not stop until breeding has taken place. The male boa will flick his tongue on the female's back while riding on her back and following her everywhere. He will also use his spurs to tickle and prick at the base of a female's tail and cloaca area. I believe that this heavy spurring and courting are what set a female up for egg development.

Copulation

Some novices will mistake courting for copulation. This is easy to misidentify as the male will usually court a female for many

Copulation in *Boa constrictor*.

weeks before actual copulation takes place. While courting he will align his tail with the female's cloaca and will try to breed with her. But with the cloacas aligned it is sometimes hard to tell if they are indeed copulating. A tell tale sign of copulation is "Tail Waving". If and when the male does copulate with the female he will lie with his tail next to the female's with one of his hemipenes inserted into her cloaca. While he is inserted he will curl his tail and wave it back and forth. This is what I look for to tell if copulation is taking place. I must also note that the actual copulation usually takes place just before ovulation and sometimes during ovulation.

Ovulation

Female boas have follicles present at any time of year. It is the non-feeding cycle, then feeding cycle and finally the temperature cycling and introduction of males that gets these follicles to grow and mature. Follicular development in boas can be quite quick in some boas and can take many months in others (all female boas are different and develop eggs on different time schedules). Follicles can be palpated in smaller races of boas and feel like small marbles, lined up in a row. It's harder to detect in larger boas as there may be too much body mass to feel these follicles. When follicles are maturing the male boas seem to be able to smell it or can tell visually by the swelling of the female. At this time most male boas will use their spurs and court the females constantly. He will do this until the female lets him copulate with her. I have had male boas that have courted females for months before they are allowed to breed. At the same time I have seen copulation within minutes of introduction. Most copulation is observed just before ovulation and I have had boas copulate many weeks before ovulation. It's my theory that the eggs are fertilized during copulation and that ovulation takes place when these fertilized eggs reach a certain maturity and are then passed through the oviduct. (This is the actual ovulation.) At ovulation a female boa exhibits a huge swelling in her abdomen. It looks as if she has eaten a huge meal. This swelling lasts approximately 24 hours and I have noticed that some boas may ovulate two times because they have two oviducts and these oviducts may ovulate a few days apart. Usually a very large ovulation is actually both oviducts ovulating in unison.

A gravid female boa.

Gravid Boas

After ovulation it is very important that a gravid boa has a proper temperature gradient to thermoregulate its body's temperature. Gravid boas will seek the warmest place in their enclosure and set there in a 'heat conservation position'. This position may look like a tightly coiled spring and this spring will tighten when it is cool and loosen when it is hot. The gravid female will also move on and off the heat to regulate her temperature. I keep my heat pads set to 92° F for my gravid boas and they usually set on them with semi-tight coils throughout the entire pregnancy. Female boas that are gravid should also have plenty of fresh clean water available at all times as the maturing babies will take up a lot of fluids from the mother. I must also note that most gravid boas will get much darker in color after their post ovulation shed. There is one theory that this darker complexion helps the female retain heat better.

Post Ovulation Shed & Gestation

Most female boas will go into a shed cycle immediately after ovulation. This shed cycle usually takes much longer than a feeding shed cycle. Most of these shed cycles are complete and the Boa sheds approximately 20 days after ovulation. I say most boas shed because I have had many female boas that have NOT shed after ovulation.

In the past, the gestation time of a boa was always exaggerated and some books represent it as being as long as 6 months. Today with more people breeding boas and keeping records we have a much better idea of the length of gestation of boas.

There are two ways of determining when your boa will give birth. The first is counting approximately 120 days after the obvious ovulation. It's even easier if your boa sheds after ovulation as you can then count approximately 105 days from this shed to determine birth. These numbers are just guidelines and there are many factors that can alter these numbers. The lack of supplemental heat can greatly slow down the process. Also – if you do not note the ovulation and there was no post ovulation shed – you may then have to guess by counting approximately 145 days from last observed copulation.

Parturition

Female boas will get quite restless a few days before giving birth. If you use a paper substrate they will constantly try to get under it so

Boa giving birth.

Newborn boas, just seconds after birth.

you can add more sheets of paper to help keep them comfortable. If you are using a bedding type product they will push it around and try to make a depression in it. Either way you should try and keep the mother comfortable. I do not recommend keeping a hide box with a gravid female as they could deliver the babies in the hide box and could end up crushing some of them.

Boas usually give birth at night or just before day break. But I have seen plenty of births in the middle of the day with all the lights on. The gravid boa will typically stretch out her body along one wall of her enclosure when contractions start. They then will start turning their body into a circle around the mass of babies as they are born. The birthing process can be very fast. I have come down to see a boa giving birth to her first baby and by the time I run to get my camera she is almost completed with the process. I have also observed many females pushing their heads into the pile of babies as if to try and disperse them or get them to break out of their amniotic sacs.

I always take the mother out of the cage when I find that she is finished delivering her young. If left with the babies she will get quite cranky and will try and strike at you to defend her litter. But if you find her just after birth she should still be calm enough to move her to a soaking tub filled with a few inches of water. This will help clean off any albumen left from the babies

Birth completed.

along with any smell left behind to remind her of the birth. I then put her in a fresh clean enclosure and leave her alone for a day then feed her a good-sized meal. She should feed ravenously at this time. Failure to feed or reluctance to do so may be a sign of retained ova or babies. If this is the case then a trip to a qualified veterinarian is in order.

As for the babies – I leave them in the enclosure in which they were born for at least two days, making sure there are no spaces small enough for a baby boa to escape from. I do this because it takes a few days for the amniotic sac to pull away from the umbilical cord. You should NEVER pull the umbilical from the sac as the baby boa may bleed to death. Therefore it is safest to leave them to pull it off as it dries and again this could take a day or two. I will also put a few sheets of wet newspaper or paper towels over the pile of babies in order to keep them moist and humid. I also will mist them down a few times a day. As soon as the babies appear that they are all out of their sacs and moving about the cage they will usually all pile up near a heat source. At this time I take them out and place them into a 28 quart Rubbermaid® tub filled with slightly moist sphagnum moss. This Rubbermaid® tub is then kept in a rack system with a heat tape in the back that is set to 90° F. The new boas will again pile up and wait to shed which is usually 7-10 days after birth. As soon as they all shed I set them up individually in shoe boxes in a rack with heat tape set to 87° F.

Infertile ova (Slugs)

Infertrile ova or slugs.

A female that is gravid with unfertilized ova will look much thinner than a female that is filled with live young. There are many compensating factors that can lead up to females giving birth to infertile ova. The number one reason is lack of proper thermal gradient. If the female cannot thermo regulate properly (get on or away from heat) the eggs will not develop properly and hence will be deposited as infertile ova. Another reason for infertile ova may be that the male simply missed the window of opportunity because he was taken out of the female's enclosure too early. And finally a third reason for this is the age of your breeders. If they are too young, they may deliver slugs as their muscle mass was not enough to handle such a taxing endeavor on the body. Infertile ova are also quite difficult to deliver as they are much drier than living young. The process could take a day or so to completely finish and often some eggs are left behind. If this is the case, a trip to a qualified veterinarian will be in order and surgery may have to be done to remove these ova.

Chapter FIVE: Genetics

Coral Albino boa.

Simple Recessive

I always found genetics interesting in high school and college and experimented often with mice to see the outcome of certain breedings. Then when I got serious about breeding snakes it seemed that all those days in Biology class started making sense. It always amazed me that the breeding results were pretty much what was to be expected based on Mendel's pea plant crosses (Tall X Short) and by using Reginald Punnett's "Punnett Square". The first trait I learned about in Biology was the *Simple Recessive* trait.

In genetics, the term "recessive gene" refers to an allele that causes a phenotype (visible or detectable characteristic) that is only seen in a homozygous genotype (an organism that has two copies of the same allele and therefore exhibits the trait). Every boa has two copies of every gene, one from its mother and one from its father. If a genetic trait is recessive, a boa needs to inherit two copies of the gene for the trait to be expressed. Thus, both parents have to be carriers of a recessive trait (heterozygous) for a boa to express that trait. If both parents are carriers, each boa born will have a 25% chance of exhibiting that recessive trait (1 in 4 should exhibit the trait). If one parent is homozygous for the trait (exhibits that trait) and the other parent is a carrier (heterozygous) for the trait, each boa born will have a 50% chance of exhibiting that recessive trait (2 in 4 should exhibit the trait). And finally if both parents are homozygous for the trait, then each boa born will have 100% chance of exhibiting the trait. I use the term " % chance of exhibiting the trait" because in large numbers these numbers work out pretty much to exactly what is expected. However, with small litters of boas the odds may be in your favor or against you. Therefore your resulting offspring have those percentages of being what you want them to be.

The most common simple recessive trait in boas is albinism (lacking melanin). Albinism in boas has proven to be a genetic simple recessive trait. This means that when you breed an albino boa to normal appearing boa, the resulting offspring will all be normal. However, all of those normal appearing offspring will be *heterozygous* for the albino gene. This means that although they appear normal, they carry the gene for albinism.

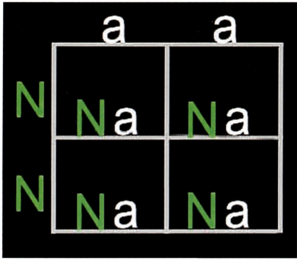

A typical Punnett Square showing the results of a cross between an Albino (aa) with a Normal animal (NN).

Incomplete Dominance

For the longest time breeders in the herpetological community have erroneously used the term "Co-dominant" when in reality they are referring to *Incomplete Dominance*. Incomplete dominance works in a similar fashion to recessive traits in that the heterozygous offspring are genes carriers for a specific trait. However, in incomplete dominance the heterozygous animals have a visual indicator and therefore are "Visually Heterozygous". This means they exhibit another type of color or pattern that is halfway between the Normal phase and the Super or more exaggerated Dominant phase. So if you breed boas to each other that are incomplete dominant and are visually heterozygous for an extreme trait, you will have a 1 in 4 chance of producing the Super or more exaggerated form which will be "Dominant". This dominant boa when bred to a Normal will then produce all or 100% of a litter of visually heterozygous offspring. And finally, if you breed these visual hets to a normal you will get 50/50 or half a litter of visual hets and half normal appearing boas.

With *Incomplete Dominance* a cross between organisms with two different phenotypes produces offspring with a third phenotype that

Super Hypo Sonoran Boa.

Arabesque Boa.

is a *blending* of both parental traits. An example of this in plants that makes it easy to remember is the crossing of a red flower (dominant) with a white flower (recessive). In incomplete dominance the results of such a cross will make all pink flowers (like mixing paint). An example of this in *Boa constrictor* is the incomplete dominant trait of hypomelanism. This trait is quite common in Central American Boas and the most popular one was popularized by Rich Ihle and named "Salmon Hypo Boa" for its underlying salmon colors. The trait is incomplete dominant in that the Super form (Exaggerated or Dominant) is very light and exhibits very little to no black color at all and the visual heterozygous form or simply named "Hypo Boa" is a little darker and appears to be visually distinguished as being something between a Normal and a Super. When this Super Hypo (the dominant or Red Flower) is bred to a normal appearing Boa (White Flower) the result is all Hypo Boas (Pink Flowers). The Hypo Boas or Pink Flowers are now heterozygous for the Super Hypo trait. However, they are a visible heterozygous boa in that they too are hypomelanistic – but not as exaggerated as the Dominant Super Form and therefore are the blend of both traits.

Co-dominance

In Co-dominance, the "recessive" and "dominant" traits appear together in the phenotype of hybrid organisms. With co-dominance, a cross between organisms with two different phenotypes produces offspring with a third phenotype in which both of the parental traits appear together.

Super Hypo Salmon Boa.

Co-dominance is pretty much the same as incomplete dominance. A hybrid organism shows a third phenotype - not the usual "dominant" one and not the "recessive" one, but a third, different phenotype. With co-dominance we get a blending of the dominant and recessive traits so that the third phenotype exhibits both traits together. An example of this in plants that makes it easy to remember is the crossing of a Red Flower (Dominant) to a White Flower. In co-dominance the results of such a cross will make a Red Flower with White Spots or stripes (not pink). I know of no such incidence in boa genetics at this time that has proven to be co-dominant. However, a few Paradox type animals have popped up from Albino to heterozygous and from a few double heterozygous breedings. These very rare resulting offspring exhibit both albinism and normal patterning/color in a single animal. Thus the name Paradox has been used for these strange anomalies. However, none have proven to be genetically reproducible.

Dominant Traits

In genetics, the term dominant gene refers to the allele that causes a phenotype that is seen in a heterozygous genotype. Every boa has two copies of every gene, one from the mother and one from the father. If a genetic trait is dominant, a boa only needs to inherit one copy of the gene for the trait to be expressed. An example of this in boas is the genetic trait called "Arabesque". This trait is dominant because when an Arabesque is bred to a normal appearing mate the resulting offspring are approximately half a litter of Arabesque and half are normal. The normal boas in these litters are not heterozygous for Arabesque, making this a dominant trait.

Chapter SEVEN: Diseases, Parasites & Disorders in *Boa constrictor*

Retained eye cap.

A whole text book of information can be written on this subject and still may not cover all aspects of maladies seen in captive boas. Therefore I will cover the most common problems with keeping boa constrictors and include as much information as possible for the average keeper to utilize to keep from running into such problems. I am also a big advocate of veterinary care and highly recommend that you align yourself with a veterinarian that has experience with reptile medicine in case you do have an ill boa. Reptile medicine has come a long way in the past ten years and vets can send cultures out to laboratories and get back information regarding the exact genus and species of the bacteria that is causing the problem. They then have a list of antibiotics that can be used to target each bacterium and stop it from growing. So you can see that if you the keeper try to stop an infection with a certain broad spectrum antibiotic, you may not be targeting the right genus or species of bacteria and could be wasting your time. Lastly I must mention the fact that by using the wrong

An albino boa with a life-threatening upper respiratory infection. Photo by Dean Wallace DVM.

antibiotic your boa is building up a resistance, also known as antimicrobial resistance or drug resistance and may be immune to it in the future.

Respiratory Infection

Upper respiratory infection is probably the most common disorder in captive Boa constrictors. This is because boa constrictors are tropical creatures and require a certain amount of heat and humidity to thrive. However, in captivity these two things may be difficult to recreate and some keepers may simply not notice that their humidity is low and that their temperatures are too low. It is these two compensating factors that lead to upper respiratory infection. I also must note that some hobbyists have killed their boas with kindness by keeping them too wet. This is a problem especially if the low temperatures are ignored and then the same results occur.. Common symptoms of upper respiratory infection are noisy, raspy breathing along with opening of the mouth and bubbling from the nose.

Some mild cases of upper respiratory infection can be treated by placing the boa in a very warm environment with a heat pad set at around 92° F. The enclosure should be a small space or unit that will keep the boa close to the heat source. You must be careful to monitor this setup because if the boa gets too hot it could die. This "Hospital" type setup should also be kept humid – but not very wet. The warm humid air within this setup along with the belly heat should boost the boa's immune system and help get it back to normal in a few weeks. No food should be offered at this time as the small space is not conducive for proper care and not enough space to defecate properly.

If a mild case is left unchecked and the boa cannot thermoregulate properly the symptoms can worsen. Such symptoms then may include constant mouth opening with a foam discharge in the corners of the mouth along with heavy fluid discharge from the nose. Since boas cannot cough to expel these mucoid secretions they may be found with their heads up in the air leaning on the side of their enclosure. They do this to try to keep the fluid from clogging their lung. However, if they get to this point it is fair to say that the lung is probably filled with fluid. At this point a visit to your local veterinarian is suggested. Some boa enthusiasts feel they can treat their animals by buying antibiotics and injecting their boas themselves. This practice has commonly lead to problems because most of the time the boa starts to improve and then the antibiotic cycle is stopped. However if the full cycle is not completed the boa may relapse or even worse it could then build up an immunity to the antibiotic and it will be that much tougher to knock out the problem with a later dosing.

Mouth Rot

This condition (AKA necrotic stomatitis) is a common malady in captive *Boa constrictor*s and could be fatal. Nervous snakes that strike against the terrarium glass and injure the mouth and jaw are susceptible to bacterial invasion of the mucous membranes in the mouth. This problem can also be caused by bedding that gets lodged in the snake's mouth. It is important to catch this disease in its early stages. Any swelling of the mouth should be investigated. The disease manifests itself in inflamed mucous membranes, with a paste-like mass adhering to areas around the teeth. This problem can be cured by cleaning the mouth, gums and teeth with a tooth brush and Listerine® mixed with water. You must make sure that you get all of the rot out of the mouth and it is a good sign to see red blood coming from the infected area (this means that you cleaned it enough to expose the good tissue). In very bad cases of mouth rot a veterinarian may be needed to prescribe an antibiotic to help fight the infection.

Some updated medical dosages that are recommended by the 2005 Merck Veterinary manual are as follows. *All of the dosages below pertain to Boa constrictor.*

Amakacin: 5 milligrams per kilogram intramuscularly for the first dose, then 2.5 milligrams per kilogram every 72 hours. This should continue throughout the clinical signs of the ailment and for a week after clinical signs end.

Your boa should be housed at the high end of the optimum temperature range during treatment. Amakacin is nephrotoxic or damaging to the kidneys. Therefore boas should be very well hydrated during treatments and food should be withheld.

This antibiotic works well on most upper respiratory infections as well as pneumonia.

Baytril (Enrofloxacin): 10 milligrams per kilogram intramuscularly for the first dose, then 5 milligrams per kilogram every 48 hours. This should continue through out the clinical signs of the ailment and for a week after clinical signs end. Administration of this product is painful and may result in tissue necrosis and sterile abscesses; may cause skin discoloration or tissue necrosis if given subcutaneous. Baytril is a broad-spectrum antibiotic that is often used to treat upper respiratory infections, oral abscesses, mouth rot and *Pseudomonas*.

Fortaz (Ceftazidime): 20 milligrams per kilogram subcutaneous or intramuscularly every 72 hours. This should continue through out the clinical signs and for a week after clinical signs end. This antibiotic is highly effective against gram-negative bacteria like *Pseudomonas*.

Gentamicin: 2.5 milligrams per kilogram intramuscularly every 72 hours. This should continue through out the clinical signs of the ailment and for a week after clinical signs end. Gentamicin is nephrotoxic or damaging to the kidneys. Therefore boas should be very well hydrated during treatments and food withheld. Hydration by injecting lactated ringers solution may be required. This antibiotic is used for upper respiratory infection and pneumonia.

***Note** - As you can see, the dosage length of time is not yet a clear cut science and therefore these dosages should be administered under the supervision of a qualified veterinarian. The information here is intended as a general guide and not to be construed as medical advice. Most severe medical conditions should be treated by a qualified veterinarian.

Inclusion Body Disease (IBD)

Inclusion Body Disease is a fatal viral disease that is more common in *Boa constrictor* than any other member of the family Boidae. This disease has been around a very long time (30+ years) and is in no way something new, especially to top boa breeders in the U.S. and abroad. IBD is also known as Boa "AIDS" because this virus is caused by a similar member of the Retrovirus family that causes human and feline AIDS. Infected boas are in reality the "host" of this virus. Symptoms of this disease are inability to right themselves, 'star gazing' or turning their heads up and back. They have a dull demeanor and inability to straighten them selves out with a contorted posture. And lastly, regurgitation or refusal to eat is symptoms of this malady.

Since IBD is a viral disorder it can only be transmitted from one boa to another via bodily fluids (breeding) or direct contact with fecal contamination (drinking water from a bowl that has feces from an infected boa.). However, the virus cannot live very long outside the host and therefore will most likely die. But strict quarantine is required for boas that are questionable hosts to this disease. It is also assumed that mites are the number one cause of the spread of this disease as they carry blood from one boa host to another. But again, more research is needed to prove this theory.

A boa with Inclusion Body Disease.

IBD also is very hard to be effectively diagnosed by a veterinarian. Veterinarians will draw blood from a suspect boa. A complete Blood Cell Count (CBC) is done to look for elevations of white blood cells, but this is not evidence of IBD because the elevated white blood cell count could simply be a natural immune defense to a viral invader which could or could not be due to IBD. It is also common for veterinarians to take a biopsy from a kidney, stomach, pancreas and brain. These biopsies could yield inclusion body results within the tissue, but again, this does not fully confirm that the boa is not infected with IBD nor does a negative diagnosis or lack of inclusion bodies mean that your boa is not infected as the biopsy could have been taken from a place with no inclusion body damage.

Therefore you can see the frustration this disease is causing. A lot of research is being done on this disorder here in the U.S. and in Europe. The hopes are that a simple blood test can be designed to diagnose this problem. But that may be many years away.
As far as a cure – there is no cure for IBD. But misdiagnoses of this disease occur when a boa may have a bacterial infection. I have even heard of boas that had kidney failure and showed these IBD

symptoms. Another misdiagnosis is caused by over heating as boas that have been exposed to extremely high temperatures will also show IBD-like symptoms.

There is one theory that all boas have these "Inclusion Bodies" in their cells and that stressful conditions can deplete the snake's immune system and therefore these inclusion bodies have an opportunity to take over. There is no scientific evidence of any of this, however it does make sense.

How can you avoid obtaining a boa with IBD? That is almost impossible to tell because this virus has also been know to lie dormant in a host for over a year while the host looks and acts completely normal. This host or carrier can breed with another boa and the other boas can get infected with the disease and show signs very quickly then die.

One very unconventional method of detecting this disease in a boa collection is the use of housing a Ball Python with a suspect boa. From what I gather it is assumed that the more susceptible Ball Python will succumb to the disease if it is present within just a few months. I personally do not know how reliable this method is, however it may be worth trying if for any reason you are suspect of any of your boas.

Quarantine is the best method of keeping this disorder in check. The second best thing to do is to eradicate any mites if they are present as they could possibly spread this disease.

Ectoparasites

Ectoparasites are parasites that live on the skin of your *Boa constrictor*. The most common ectoparasite is the snake mite *(Ophionyssus natricis)*. This tiny arachnid causes problems by sucking the blood of their host, causing skin problems, aggravating and disturbing the host and by transmitting serious diseases from the mite to the reptile. Mites are very small and almost invisible as youngsters. As adults they are black and look like poppy seeds. They are also about the same size as poppy seeds and have tiny legs. A mite that is full of blood will pop when crushed and therefore easy

Mite-infested boa. Note the mites around the eye.

to distinguish. In addition mites can be very difficult to eliminate once they are introduced to a captive snake collection. According to a report written by Dave and Tracy Barker of VPI, at 86º F a gravid engorged female mite looking for a place to lay eggs can travel at a speed of up to 20 cm per minute, up to 12 metres in an hour, and they may travel several hours looking for a good place to deposit eggs. Unfed females can crawl up to a rate of 28 cm per minute - almost 17 metres per hour. Therefore you can see how quickly this problem spreads.

How to avoid getting mites in the first place: Snakes coming from the wild have a good chance of carrying ectoparasites and so do captive born boas from private breeders. Mites have been a long time problem in boa keeping simply because mites spread quickly from one snake to another by traveling. They can climb vertical areas with no problem and colonize a boa collection in a very short time. Therefore you should quarantine each and every snake you bring into your facility or snake room (even if mites are not visibly present). I do this by putting the snake in a room other than my snake room and soak it in a shallow tub of warm water with a tight lid. I then spray the snake (while it's soaking) with a solution of Nix®. This product is used against head lice in children and is a

Pyrethrin-based product that is quite safe to boas. I use 2 ounces of Nix® per 16 ounces of water. This is placed in a spray bottle and used to spray and cover the snakes back while soaking. This kills all mites that will try and get to the top of the snake to avoid the water and it is known to kill the eggs too. I leave the quarantined boa to soak for an hour or so then put him a snake rack that is *not* in my snake room. I continue this process one week later to ensure I have killed all mites and eggs.

Mites in a water dish.

I also avoid visiting other people's collections and pet shops that have or are known for having mites as these mites can travel on you and could get into your collection inadvertently.

How do I get rid of mites once I see them? The same strategy used above works well. Soak mite-infested Boas in a tub of warm water for at least two hours. Mites cannot swim and will drown in water. During this time spray the snake and the lid of the tub with Nix® (2 ounces Nix® to 16 ounces water) in copious amounts to kill any living mites. The snake is then placed in a quarantine unit with newspaper substrate and I continue the soaking and spraying with Nix® process every 4 days for two weeks. The next step in this problem is cleaning the snakes unit from which he came from. This cage or unit will have mites and eggs in it. The shelving you keep your units on will also have mites and eggs on them. It is highly recommended that you take the unit outside and hose it down. Then use a bleach/water solution and scrub the entire unit. You should do the same for your shelving and I would advise that you mop the floor near and around the snakes unit or vacuum (if you have a rug) with moth balls in the vacuum bag to kill any sucked up mites. This process should be repeated in a weak to 9 days as unfound mite eggs could hatch in that time.

Mites can also be deterred and controlled by using a few commercially made products. One such product called "Provent A Mite®" can be used as a prophylactic as it can be used to create a barrier that mites will not cross. This product comes in an aerosol type can and can be sprayed on the cage furniture, the cage floor and most importantly the cage vents and perimeter of the openings. This product is not meant to be sprayed on the snake directly.

The easiest way of deterring mites in a captive environment is to keep a tub of water in you boas enclosure at all times. This tub should be large enough for your boa to fully submerge its body. Your boa will soak itself if mites start to take over. The mites then will drown and the life cycle interrupted. The mites simply cannot get a strong hold if they cannot suck blood from your boa.

Another ectoparasite that may be a pest on wild-caught boas is the tick. Ticks engorge themselves on the blood of a host (your boa) and cause a lot of stress. Luckily, ticks are easy to see and can be taken off manually with tweezers, ensuring that the mouthparts are removed as well. Also, ticks would be much more common on a wild-caught boa and rarely (if ever) on captives. I have seen many boas from the wild with large ticks on them. The most common place for these parasites is just below the head. This is a common place because the boa may soak in water to relieve the pressure from these parasites. However, the boa must keep its head above the water and hence the ticks simply move upward towards the head to stay out of the water. Therefore you may see some serious scarring around the necks of some wild-caught boas.

Endoparasites

Endoparasites are internal parasites that live inside the host and colonize in organs such as the intestines, lung and liver. Endoparasites are most likely present in all boas to a certain extent and most of the time the host lives a completely normal life and coexist with the few endoparasites that may be present. However, under stress these endoparasites can take over the host's intestinal tract to the point that infection could set in and rapidly lead to death. The most common problem and first signs of an infestation are regurgitation because the boa cannot digest its food properly. Other initial signs of severe parasite (nematodes, tapeworms, flukes, etc.) infection include loss of appetite, emaciation, and the presence of worms, their eggs, or segments of tapeworms in the feces. Routine microscopic examination of feces samples by a qualified veterinarian will provide evidence of infection and what type of parasite is present. These nematodes and other endoparasites can be treated with oral Fenbendazole (Panacur) at 50-100 Mg/Kg once daily for 3-5 days.

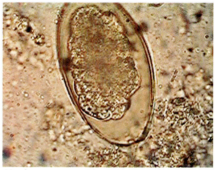
Hookworm ova. Photo by Dean Wallace, DVM.

In captive-born boas regurgitation can also become a problem if a boa is stressed or kept under sub optimum conditions like low temperatures. Boas also can get intestinal flagellates which cause regurgitation and diarrhea. Intestinal flagellates can take over a boa's intestines in time of stress or unsanitary conditions. It is important to keep your boa's water bowl clean at all times because if a boa drinks water that is stagnant or has feces in it, it could be susceptible to these intestinal flagellates. It is also important to clean up feces as soon as possible because Cryptosporium oocysts can survive for several months in your boa enclosure. These oocysts can then be ingested and the evil cycle repeats itself. These protozoans can be treated with oral Metronidazole (Flagyl) at 50-100Mg/Kg once, and then repeat in a week.

Regurgitation

The most common regurgitation problem in captive-born boas is caused by over feeding. Boas that are overfed cannot digest their food quickly enough and eventually will begin to regurgitate their meals. I cannot emphasize enough how important a proper feeding regimen and water bowl cleaning is to the health of your boa.

The Subspecies of *Boa constrictor*

Boa constrictor amarali
Bolivian Boa

Boa constrictor amarali was described in 1932 in a paper titled "Five New Subspecies of the Family Boidae" by Olive Griffith Stull. She chose the subspecies name *amarali* in honor of Dr. Afranio do Amaral, director of the Instituto Butantun in Sao Paulo, Brazil – he was the collector of the holotype specimen and a few paratype specimens used to describe this subspecies. The paratypes that were studied came from the following geographic areas: Sao Paulo, Brazil – Santa Cruz, Bolivia and Matto Grosso, Brazil. Therefore *Boa c. amarali* typically occurs throughout the Pantanal, Cerrado and Atlantic rainforest habitats from 13° LS in Brazil throughout the same habitats in Bolivia down to Paraguay, with its southern limit in Paraguay at the Tropic of Capricorn. This subspecies is sandwiched between *Boa c. constrictor* to the north and *Boa c. occidentalis* to the south and west in Argentina and Paraguay. The natural habitat of *amarali* in Paraguay has been almost completely wiped out by clear cutting for soy plantations. *B. c. amarali*, which does not occur in

Argentina but in Paraguay, is ironically more threatened than *occidentalis* which are C.I.T.E.S Appendix I and also occur in Paraguay.

The habitat of *amarali* includes rainforest, savannahs, and woodlands where it rains heavily most of the year. Since Bolivia is south of the equator the summer or rainy season is from November to March with December being the wettest month. The winter or dry season is from May to October with July being the coolest month with temperatures as low as the high 50's F at night.

Stull described *Boa c. amarali* as having 71–79 dorsal scale rows at mid body, 226–237 ventral Scales, 43–52 subcaudal scales and 22 dorsal saddles snout to vent.

She described the dorsum as being pale and the belly coloration as being "uniformly heavily gray-speckled". I have seen captive *amarali* with dark speckled bellies that ranged from dark brown to red to dark charcoal gray with a dorsum color of pale red to pink and commonly gray. I believe that the pink / red *amarali* of today are more of a product of selective breeding. Stull also pointed out the fact that the holotype had 22 dorsal saddles from snout to vent and 5 tail saddles. In the description she verifies that the largest specimen observed was just over 5 feet or 1570 mm. These boas are a small subspecies compared to their neighbors to the north and south and max out at around 6 feet or so. And finally Stull described the connected and extremely pointed widow's peaks on the back that faded into the short tail to become quadrangular in shape. This attribute is still very identifiable in captive *amarali* today.

Boa constrictor constrictor
True Red-Tailed Boas

In the past the genus Boa has been juggled between assignments of Boa and Constrictor, simply because of irresolvable differences in opinion as to the systematic relationship between *Boa constrictor* and *Corallus caninus* (which was formerly known as *Boa caninius*). To begin, The genus name of Boa and the species name of constrictor (creating the full species *Boa constrictor*) were described in 1758 by Carl Linnaeus in a pamphlet titled "Systema Naturae". His original type locality for the species *Boa constrictor* was referred to as being from India. We now know that he was referring to the Caribbean "West Indies" and that it was an error. However, I cannot discredit Linnaeus as he updated his "Systema Naturae" constantly. As time went on and more specimens and information came available Linnaeus updated this work and in later volumes he noted the distribution of *Boa constrictor* as being

Striped Guyana Boa, *Boa constrictor constrictor.*

Mexico to Argentina and the Antilles.

In 1768 Laurenti changed the genus name of Boa to Constrictor in a paper Titled "Synopsin Reptilium". The distribution was also noted as Mexico to Argentina and the Antilles. This then made the full species name, *Constrictor constrictor.*

Although the genus and species names were changed a few times between the late 1700s and mid 1900s, thanks to Lother Forcart we get a final assignment of *Boa constrictor constrictor* and this was published in Herpetologica 1951 (more about this is mentioned in the Chapter on "Taxonomy"). The distribution he notes is "Amazonian South America to Argentina and Paraguay and Trinidad and Tobago". This is the boa we commonly call True Red-Tailed Boa or Amazon Basin Boa.

The scale counts are as follows and pertain to all *Boa c. constrictor* in this section: Mid body scale rows 77-95, ventral scales 231-250, subcaudal scales 43-62 and dorsal saddles 14-22.

Boa constrictor imperator
Central American Boa

Boa constrictor imperator is the most commonly kept boa in the pet trade today. Some names given to these boas are "Central American Boa", "Common Boa" or "Colombian Red-Tailed Boa". Although many common boa constrictors do have pretty red tails, they are not **true** Red Tailed Boas. The True Red-Tailed Boas are *Boa constrictor constrictor* found east of the Andes Mountains in South America and have much redder tails.

For the past 25 years thousands of Boas have been imported annually from Colombia and the Central American countries of Nicaragua, Honduras, Panama and El Salvador as farm bred baby boas, with the majority of these Boas coming from Colombia, South America and Nicaragua, Central America. These babies are born from wild caught gravid females that are kept on the farms until they deliver their young. As soon as they are born and all export documentation is finalized – the mass export to The U.S. commences. The Boas from these exportations represent a large number of the vast population of Boas that are maintained as pets and breeders here in the United States today. Sadly, these mass exports of Boas will not last forever due to some over collecting and more importantly, deforestation of rainforest. Luckily hundreds of Boas are also captive bred here in the United States by responsible boa breeders and these captive bred and born boas may be the only way of obtaining stock in the future. I must emphasize the fact that the greatest compensating factor in the demise of Boa constrictors in the wild will not be from over collecting – but from mass destruction of habitat.

Boa imperator was described by Daudin in 1803. It was described as having 55 – 79 mid body dorsal scales rows; 225 – 260 ventral scales; 47 – 70 subcaudal scales and 22 – 30 dorsal saddles from snout to vent. Daudin placed the type locality of *imperator* to Cordoba, Veracruz, Mexico then in 1950 Smith and Taylor extended the range to Veracruz, Mexico then also in 1950 Dunn and Saxe extended the range to Chaco, Colombia. And finally in 1951, Forcart designated it as *Boa constrictor imperator*.

Today we identify the range of *Boa c. imperator* as Sonora Mexico south through Central America to extreme northwest Venezuela, northern Colombia then further south down the west coast of South America to north west Ecuador. The subspecies *Boa c. imperator* has the second largest range of *Boa constrictor* (first being *Boa c. constrictor*). *Boa c. imperator* only occur on the west side of the Andes Mountains and should not be confused with the larger true Red-Tailed Boas *(Boa c. constrictor)* which occur east of the Andes. The mainland form of *Boa c. imperator,* inhabit areas which vary from desert lowlands to tropical rainforest to high elevation cloud forests. The insular form of *Boa c. imperator* occurs on the Pacific and Caribbean sides of Central America and Mexico where they inhabit many small coastal islands which are remnant continental and volcanic uplift islands. *Boa c. imperator* also inhabits small cays (sometimes pronounced keys) on the Caribbean side of Central America. Cays are sandy islands witch may consist of Mangrove Forests and little fresh water. These sandy islands were formed by coral reefs that were exposed during low tides. Mangrove tree seeds took root on these reefs and eventually formed these cays after thousands of years.

Mexican Boa, *Boa constrictor imperator*.

With such diversity within a single subspecies, some herpetologists in the past have tried recognizing a few of these island forms as separate subspecies. However in order to be recognized as a separate subspecies an animal must have genetic isolation from the mainland species. Therefore most Central American, island boas - with the exceptions of *Boa c. nebulosus*, *Boa c. orophias* and B*oa c. sabogae*, are all considered *Boa c. imperator* because the distance from their island habitat to the mainland was not sufficient for determination of reproductive isolation. However, it is important to understand that even though the boas from this large range are all considered one subspecies, they are all truly identifiable due to geography, elevation and evolutionary changes in their environment. Thus I find it important to keep the different localities of *imperator* pure. For example, the chances of a Hog Island Boa breeding with a mainland Panamanian Boa are highly unlikely to occur in the wild.

Colombian Boa, *Boa constrictor imperator*.

Colombia is a "Melting Pot" country in South America when it comes to its herpetofaunal diversity. This is probably because Colombia is bordered by Panama to its north, Ecuador to its southwest, Peru to its south, Brazil to its southeast and Venezuela to its east. All of these political borders mean nothing to fauna and flora and therefore the biodiversity is extraordinary here in Colombia. The northern Andes region is one of the most biologically diverse areas on the planet. The Pacific and Caribbean coasts encompass a diversity of environments, flanked by the Chocó on the Pacific and a variety of dry ecosystems on the Atlantic. Inland, the Andes Mountains spread in several ranges with complex geological histories, resulting in a number of endemic plant and animal species. Further inland on the Colombia-Venezuela frontier there are savannas, and further to the east, the Orinoco basin. A network of rivers originating in the northern Andes forms the headwaters of the northeastern Amazon basin and this links the Andes to Amazonia.

There are two subspecies of boa that are indigenous to Colombia and they are *Boa c. imperator* and *Boa c. constrictor*. The Andes Mountains run through Colombia with *Boa c. imperator* being found to the west of the Andes and *Boa c. constrictor* to the east. In these pages we will discuss the more commonly exported Boa - *Boa c. imperator*.

The common Colombian Boa constrictor *(Boa c. imperator)* has been exported to the U.S. in very large numbers for the past 25 years. In the earlier years of exportation (early 1970s) thousands of wild-caught Colombian boas were shipped to the U.S. But in 1975 this all changed when CITES (Convention on the International Trade of Endangered Species) regulations went into affect. The convention stated that all boas are considered threatened and are to be listed as Appendix II animals in CITES law. These Appendix animals require permits to be imported or exported between countries. The status of Appendix II means that these animals are potentially threatened, but commerce can take place if shipments are accompanied by authorizing documents from the Country of Export. Drafted in 1973 and put into effect in 1975, CITES requires that some countries return 10% of all "farmed" hatchlings along with their mothers back to the place they were originally captured. However it is unlikely that the farmers abide to these laws as the adult snakes fetch a high price and usually end up in the skin trade. Currently CITES requires that Colombia can only export boas from a "Legally Established Captive Breeding Operation". Just recently the numbers of imported Colombian Boas have started to dwindle and this may be due to the fact that farmers are not reintroducing females and babies back into the wild and that there are not too many " Established Captive Breeding Operations". However, the main reason for any lack of boas is much more likely due to deforestation.

As recently as 1993 the export quota for boas from Colombia was over 40,000 live animals (this number does not include skin trade animals). But in a few years the quota was lowered to less than 6,500 live boas in 2001. Consequently in 2003 the quota was raised to 18,000 live animals but it is not known for sure if that quota was filled. I highly doubt it as I have seen less and less "farmed" Colombian boas in the pet trade in the past five years. Some commonly used names for these boas are (Past and Present); Common Boa - Colombian Red Tailed Boa – Colombian Boa – Red Tailed Boa – *Boa rubricauda* and *Boa constrictor*.

Colombian *Boa c. imperator* can be large and robust boas with some mature females exceeding 8 feet in length. On average females can get to around 7 feet and males about 5-6 feet in length There is one theory about the large size of the mainland Colombian *Boa c. imperator* and that is the fact that the ranges of *Boa c. constrictor* (True Red Tailed Boas found east of the Andes) and *Boa c. imperator* (Common Boas found west of the Andes) overlap in the northern portion of Colombia. The Andes Mountains are too high for boas to pass over and have always been the natural barrier between the two subspecies. However, the Andes mountain range starts to lose altitude in the middle of Colombia and it is here that the two subspecies co-mingle. The results are beautifully colored Common Boas, *Boa c. imperator,* with some influences of *Boa c. constrictor* in the form of size and some tail color. Colombian *imperator* have on average of 22 dorsal saddles from snout to vent and can be quite colorful with dark orange to maroon colored tails with a buck skin to yellow / brown background color. They are probably one of the most variable localities of boa and I think this is because of their close proximity to *Boa c. constrictor.*

Barranquilla

A few locality types from northern Colombia have been marketed in the past. One particularly beautiful race comes from Barranquilla, Colombia. Barranquilla is on the northern coast of Ecuador and the boas here represent some of the most colorful Boa constrictors around. These Boas average 22 strongly connected wide saddles with almost perfect circles between them. The tails have many bright red saddles and have a strong tendency to have square-shaped saddles. These boas are the perfect example of what a natural cross between the two subspecies of *constrictor* and *imperator* would look like. Their scale counts also are quite different from pure blooded *imperator* and I have counts from one female that are as follows. Ventral Scales = 250, Subcaudal Scales = 59, Mid Body scale rows = 90. Another locality race comes from the Rio Magdalena Valley in North Central Colombia. The boas here are beautiful with a lot of red undertones in their background color. The saddles do not connect as strongly but they too have the almost perfect circles between their saddles. Both of these races are definitely not as common as the pet shop "Colombian Boa" that is exported in such great numbers. However, they do enter the trade at least once every few years.

Colombian *Boa c. imperator* makes an excellent pet that is very calm which is the number one reason why they are so popular in the pet trade today. Through selective breeding, many different color phases and pattern anomalies have become available from breeders today. All of the following have derived from Colombian *Boa c. imperator* stock.

Color & Pattern Anomalies

Albino Boas – Albinism is a genetic condition that causes a lack of pigment. Albinos have little or no pigment. This is a simple recessive trait. The albino boa has some pigment in the form of red and yellow xanthophores that intensify with age. However, they are true albinos with red eyes and are one of the most sought after boas in the trade today. The first albino boas came onto the scene in 1983 when a West Coast enthusiast obtained five young albino specimens from a farm in Colombia. These boas were meticulously raised and taken care of but never bred or produced any albino boas. So the owner decided to sell two of the albino males. Pete Kahl and Paul Miles of Maryland Reptile Breeders purchased the two males in 1989 and had luck in breeding one male to a few normal females. As more luck would have it the very first heterozygous offspring were born in the summer of 1992 and the rest is history. Today this original strain of albino boa is quite strong and through more selective breeding will become even more spectacularly colored in future generations. A selectively bred color variant of this original strain albino was started by Pete Kahl and he refers to them as "Coral Albino Boas". These boas have a lot of red on their heads and bodies. The saddles exhibit far more red than a normal albino and the tails are very red. Since this appearance is a product of selective breeding it is not a reliable trait. Meaning if you breed a Coral Albino to a normal Albino you will not get heterozygous for Coral. Instead you may get some Coral looking boas from such a litter or no Corals at all. The best chances are from selectively line breeding the trait to create better and better generations of Coral Albinos. Albino Boas have also been mixed with Hypo Boas (Salmon and Orange Tails) to create Sunglow Boas = Albino Hypos.

Albino *Boa constrictor imperator.*

The albino gene has also been mixed into the Surinam *Boa c. constrictor* creating cross breeds that are sometime indistinguishable from a pure Suriname Boa. The first such breeding was done by Brian Sharp of Brian Sharp Reptiles when in 1996 he bred a Suriname Boa to an original strain albino boa. The result was a small litter of normal appearing crosses (boas with both Suriname and Colombian attributes). Brian bred these crosses in 1999 to each other to create the first albino boas that were 50 % Suriname Boa and 50% Colombian. The result was a spectacularly colored Red-tailed Albino.

NOTE: I do not recommend creating such crosses as it dilutes the true locality boas bloodlines and also creates crossbreeds that are virtually indistinguishable from their locality parent. This in turn could help unscrupulous dealers and breeders misrepresent a boa (due to its similar appearance) to a potential buyer that may be looking for a particular locality boa.

Sharp Strain Albino Boas – Another form of albinism that IS NOT compatible with the original (Pete Kahl) strain. This strain originated from a single female boa that was exported from Colombia in March of 1991. A Florida importer received it and sold it to Brian Sharp of Brian Sharp Reptiles, VA. Brian first bred this female to a heterozygous for Original Strain Albino male in 1993. The result was all normal appearing offspring (Het for the Sharp Strain and possible het for original strain). Brian then bred an offspring male back to its mother in 1995 to create the first Sharp Albinos. These boas are more orange than the original strain and exhibit a bit more color on the dorsum and saddles. Sharp Albino Boas have also been mixed with Hypo Boas (Salmon and Orange Tails) to create Sharp Sunglow Boas = Albino Hypos.

T+ Albino Boas - The "T" in T+ refers to the presence of the enzyme Tyrosinase whose presence is necessary for the production of melanin. The process of creating melanin is fairly simple. The amino acid Tyrosine is converted into Dopa and then into Dopaquinone in the presence of Tyrosinase, which is synthesized by the melanophores. This is a very simplified version of the basis for the terms Tyrosinase Positive (T+). In the (T+) albino, Tyrosinase is produced but is blocked from gaining access to the melanophores. In other words, all the ingredients are there, they are just unable to mix.

"Sharp" Albino Boa.

The first Caramel-Albino boas were born at a pet shop in Texas in 1997. The litter consisted of two Caramel-Albino females and 18 normal Boas. The parents were two completely normal looking Colombian boas. The breeding was not a planned event and the pet shop owners did not know that these boas were gene carriers for such an anomaly. This was the very first time that this particular trait appeared – anywhere. Dave and Tracy Barker of VPI purchased the entire litter. In 2000 one of the T+ Albino Boas was bred to its normal-colored sibling. She produced a litter of nine healthy babies, six caramel-albinos and three that were normal in appearance. This breeding demonstrated that the appearance was inheritable, but it could not identify the pattern of inheritance with certainty. So in 2002, Dave and Tracy successfully bred two normal-appearing siblings from the original clutch. This pairing produced a litter of 28 babies, eight caramel-albinos and twenty normal baby boas. Because a T+ Albino was produced by breeding two normal gene carriers, it was then clear that this trait was exhibited as simple recessive.

Anerythristic Boas (Anery) – Another rare recessive trait – anerythristic boas are lacking all red pigment. This creates a gray boa with white and black markings. Every year a few anerythristic boas would come into the country from the farms in Colombia. One breeder on the west coast named Glen Carlzen started line breeding these anery boas to see if the trait was genetic. In the late eighties he proved the genetics to be simple recessive and the first captive-born anerythristic boas were on the market. Some anerythristic boas keep the gray pastel on ivory white color while others tend to brown out a bit. Thus the lighter colored gray and pastel animals fetch a higher price.

Snow Boas (Anerythristic & Albino) – A double recessive, the Snow Boa is both anerythristic (lacking red) and albino. This "Man-Made" boa is snow white with pearl white highlights and red eyes at birth. However as they mature they tend to get more yellow but still lack the red tail. The first breeding was done by Pete Kahl. He produced the first Snow Boas in 1996 by breeding double heterozygous for albino and anerythristic boas (normal appearing but carried both genes). When bred to each other the chances were 1 in 16 in getting a Snow Boa and he did.

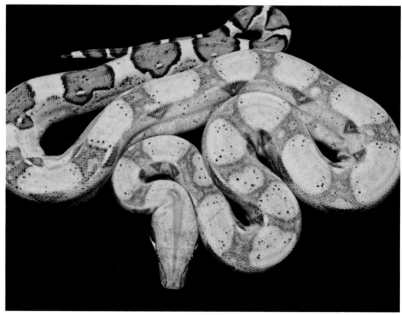
Anerythristic Boa.

There is one rare byproduct from a particular double het snow breeding done by Ralph Davis in 1999. This breeding produced what was to be expected (Snows, Albinos, Anerythristics, and Normals). However, one of the hatchlings was born as a Paradox of both the albino and anerythristic genes as it exhibited both anerythristic and albino colors within the one snake (The genes simply did not commingle – but rather separated and thus the Paradox was born). Ralph named this anomaly "The Freak". This snake looks like a Snow Boa with hints of Anerythtrism and Albinism showing through. One eye is red like an albino and the other is dark like an Anerythristic. To date it's the only occurrence of such a rare event and this type of boa has not been duplicated yet.

Arabesque Boas – A dominant gene that is a pattern anomaly. This odd pattern anomaly popped up serendipitously in a litter of normal Colombian Boas that were owned by Steve Hammond in the summer of 1989. To have a spontaneous gene mutation such as this is a very rare event - but it does occur. These boas are very unique with a boldly marked pattern with dark, thin saddles that connect the whole way down the back. The tail has very few blotches and is

Arabesque Boa.

often dark (rather than red or orange). This trait has been mixed with Hypo (Salmon and Orange Tail) and Albino.

Motley Boas – Another dominant gene. But in the case of the Motley it is an incomplete dominant trait and is the visual heterozygous form of the Super Motley which is a uni-colored black – brown boa. The Motley boa is a unique morph with circles down the back that are connected within a stripe. They are much darker in over all color compared to normal Colombian boas. This trait originated in the wild from two different locations. One was imported from Colombia in 1994 and the other from Central America. It is not known whether the two traits are allelic but it is most likely as they are very similar. The first Motleys produced in captivity were bred by Ron St. Pierre. The first Central American Motley was produced by Alex Barreiro. This trait has been mixed with Hypo (Salmon and Orange Tail) and Albino.

Jungle Boas – First produced by Lars Brandle of Sweden. This trait is also co-dominant and popped up in a breeding of a large Zig Zag patterned boa (purchased from a Zoo in Sweden) to a normal

Motley Boa. Photo by Nathan Hanks.

appearing Colombian boas in Sweden. The result was half a litter of Jungle Patterned boas. He then bred Jungle back to the Zig Zag parent and produced the first Super Jungle Boas. This trait is a Pattern / color anomaly. Most Jungles exhibit a clean background color with strong circles and saddles. The Supers are very aberrant and exhibit some striping and zig zagging with strong yellows and oranges.

Pastel Boas – The Pastel Boa project was started by Jeff Ronne as a selectively bred light-colored Colombian boa with virtually no black on the tail. He selectively bred his lightest and brightest colored boas for multiple generations to better the color and take away the darkness or melanin. Thus the result was a spectacularly colored Colombian boa with a beautiful red tail and hardly any black. Another result of this breeding is the fact that these boas stay light colored into adulthood. The name " Pastel " has been abused in the past by breeders that want to market nicely colored Colombians, but the original Pastels are boas that are produced by Jeff Ronne. The trait seems to be a recessive genetic characteristic which works like skin color in humans. Lighter skin color is a recessive trait but not simple recessive like blue eyes are for instance to brown eyes. Each generation gets better and better.

Dutch Pastel Boa. Photo by Freek Nuyt.

Dutch Pastel – This trait was started by my friend Freek Nuyt in Holland. His Pastel boa was created much in the same way as Jeff Ronne's in that he selectively bred red colored boas that had little black coloration to them. He also added to the mix a Suriname *Boa c. constrictor* to boost the red color. This color morph acts like a dominant trait in that the many successive generations are creating a strong tendency towards the reds and hypo (lacking black) colors and the babies from this bloodline are born pink to red and the color intensifies with each shed. This bloodline has produced some Hypo Pastels and Freek thinks that the Hypo Pastels are the homozygous form of the Pastel (heterozygous) gene. More breeding will determine exactly what this trait is capable of doing. It is quite rare in the U.S. and only a few examples have been exported to the U.S.

Striped Line Boas – Another morph that was started by Pete Kahl of PK Reptiles. This particular trait is genetic recessive and produces boas with beautifully striped tails and partially striped bodies. Pete started this line with a pair of striped adult Colombian boas in 1991. When he bred these boas together he got a whole litter of striped boas (proving it genetic). It seems that the degree of striping is random in this gene as some are completely striped from head to tail and some are partially striped. The red on the tails of this morph is a very intense blood red color. The bodies seem a bit darker than most Colombian boas and the result when mixed with albino creates very dark, rich-colored orange Albinos with very red tails. This gene is a great ingredient to mix into other morphs and has proven to be very valuable in boa collections.

Scoria boa- The Scoria Boa is a unique almost patternless boa that popped up serendipitously from a breeding of two normal appearing Colombian boas. It was produced in North Dakota and it is named after a rock found in North Dakota as the originator thought it kind of looked like the rock. Genetics are not known at this time.

Kubsch Pastels – The Kubsch Pastel Boas *(Pronounced Coops)* originated in Germany by a man named Sylvio Kubsch. These beautifully colored Colombian boas originated from a pair of pure Colombian boas that were related to each other. Most of the litter were amazing looking Pastel Boas and were spread to a small number of breeders in Europe. These boas like all the other Pastel lines act like a dominant trait in that when bred to unrelated animals produce some Pastel-like offspring. I think that these strong colored genes simply over ride the dull natural colors and hence more Pastel like boas are produced. However, the Kubsh Pastel gene has proven to be quite potent and some of the most orange and red Pastels have been created by these boas. The saddles on these boas are dark brown with a lot of orange highlights. They have almost perfect circles down their backs and the sides are blazing orange and the head is an orange/red. The tails are a crimson red with orange highlights. One byproduct of certain breeding of these boas in Germany is another trait called "Square Tailed Boa".

Square Tailed Boa – The Square Tailed Boas are an offshoot of the Kubsch Pastel. They were produced in Europe by a breeder that bred two Kubsch Pastels to each other and produced a few of these Square Tailed Boas. The Square Tails are unique in that they have the same pastel color as the Kubsch Pastel but have a very thin lined pattern of saddles. These thin saddles connect down the back and the tail blotches look like squares – hence the name. The genetic basis of this trait is still in question as not a lot of breeding has been done with it yet. However, there is some genetic basis around this boas as it is reproducable.

Boa constrictor longicauda
Long-tailed Boa

Boa c. longicauda was described in 1991 by Dr. Robert Price and my brother Paul Russo in a Japanese scientific journal called " The Snake". The title of the description is "Revisionary Comments on the Genus Boa with the Description of a New Subspecies of *Boa Constrictor* from Peru ".

When we first obtained a shipment of these boas from Tumbes, Peru back in 1988 we were confident that they were a new subspecies. We chose to base our determination on the more conservative scientific rule that two populations of boa are subspecifically different if they differ in character by the degree of at least 75% (full species differ by 100%). These boas definitely were very different from their neighbors (*B. c. ortonii* to the south *B. c. imperator* to the north) and greatest compensating factor in proving the validity of the subspecies *Boa c. longicauda* was that they are geographically isolated from these other subspecies by the Gulf of Guayaquill to its north, The Andes Mountains to the east, The Pacific Ocean to the west and a dry desert to its south. The name *Boa c. longicauda* was used to describe this boa because when we first received them we noticed a male courting a large female. The male's hemipenes (sexual organs) were fully everted and appeared much larger than any other Boas that we had ever seen. We then decided to probe the males to see how deep the probe would go into a hemipene. Our findings were very interesting in that male *longicauda* probed as deep as 38 subcaudal scales. Other male boa probe lengths we found in literature and from probing experiments we did ourselves were as follows; *imperator* = 23 and *constrictor* = 28. The *longicauda* probe depth represented 14.1% of the total body length, compared to 11.9% in *constrictor* this was a significant finding and since we could not name the Boa *"Boa constrictor hemipenis elongatus"* for obvious reasons – we went with *Boa c. longicauda* or Long-Tailed Boa.

The natural range of *Boa c. longicuada* is Tumbes, Peru. Its range probably extends a little further north into Manabi Province, Ecuador. As I have seen a picture in the book "Serpientes de Ecuador" which plates a boa found in Ecaudor that is identical in looks to the Tumbes Boa. The first group of *Boa c. longicauda* entered the U.S. in 1988 in a shipment from Peru. This shipment had a dozen 4 to 5 foot long adults which ranged from dark black with gray heads to all black with blue heads. Some were completely jet black with an iridescence that covered their black shiny scales. They had 19 – 21 dorsal saddles from snout to vent, 60 – 76 dorsal scale rows at mid body, 223-247 ventral scales, 60-67 subcaudal scales in males and 50-54 subcaudal scales in females. The saddles were block like and some had connected saddles and some did not. Their tails were jet black with cream colored dashes in them. The sides were a steel gray to blue and they were in my opinion one of the most unique creatures I had ever seen. One more interesting fact about these boas was the scars. Every boa in this shipment from Tumbes had huge scars on them. We assumed they were from rats or some kind of native rodent because every one of those wild caught boas ate domestic rats with gusto. From that point forward only a few shipments of these rare boas arrived in the hands of U.S. collectors. These boas are highly variable and no two look alike.

Boa constrictor nebulosus
Dominican Boa

Boa constrictor nebulosus is probably the rarest of the boa constrictors in captivity in the U.S. I personally have only seen a single living specimen in captivity and that was about 10 years ago. This rare boa inhabits the Island of Dominica (pronounced Dom-in-neeka) in the Caribbean which is part of the Lesser Antilles. The island of Dominica has been confused with the island of the Dominican Republic by some boa enthusiasts in the past and it should be noted that these are two very different places. This unique boa was first mentioned in 1931 in a book written by Raymond Ditmars "Snakes of the World". In this book, he referred to two Boas that inhabit St. Lucia and Dominica as "West Indian Boas", *Constrictor orphias*. They were also mentioned again in 1935 by Olive Griffith Stull in "A Check list of the Family Boidae" as she also referred to the boas from both St. Lucia and Dominica (Both Lesser Antilles) as *Constrictor orophias*. And finally in 1964 James D. Lazell described this Dominica boa as a separate subspecies called *Constrictor*

*constrictor nebulosus (*now known as *Boa c. nebulosus).* In his description he used the name "nebulosus" to describe the poorly defined or "nebulous" dorsal pattern of which this snake has 31-35 obscure and irregular dorsal markings on a clouded gray to brown background color. They have 258-273 ventral scales (a very high number compared to all of the other *Boa constrictor*) and 59-69 mid body scale rows. They can reach 4-6 feet long in males and 6-8 feet for females. Males are quite lighter in color to females and some large females could be jet black. Dominica is a volcanic uplift island that has very unique fauna and flora. The boas here are very genetically isolated and interbreeding does not occur. Some believe that *nebulosus* should and could be elevated to its own species. One evolutionary theory is that these boas are undergoing speciation right now.

The locals on Dominica refer to these boas as "Tet Chien" which is French for "dog head". These boas have a unique characteristic in that they den up in hollows of logs, under rocks and in undercuts created by streams (similar to North American rattlesnakes). All of these dens are within the vicinity of hot springs and sulfur gas vents created by the volcano. The reason for this habit is not totally understood because no breeding has been witnessed at these sites and the boas can be found there all year round. The climate in Dominica is quite warm in the daytime, however at night it drops to the mid sixties. Maybe this congregation is an evolutionary characteristic to conserve heat at night. More research is needed to find out.

Locals on this island are fearful of this snake as the neighboring islands of Martinique and St. Lucia have lance head vipers (*Bothrops*) and they fear getting bitten (even though Boas are not venomous) therefore they often kill them on the spot. Locals also fear the snakes as they invade hen houses.

To my knowledge there are only 3 U.S. captive births of these rare boas in captivity. Terry Vandeventer collected 5.5 boas with C.I.T.E.S. permission in 1990. Three of the females which had temperature cycled in the wild, bred in captivity and gave birth in Terry's care. These captive born *nebulosus* may very well be the only captives in U.S. collections today.

Boa c. occidentalis
Argentine Boa

Argentinian Boa, *Boa constrictor occidentalis*. Photo by Nathan Hanks.

The Argentine Boa, *Boa c. occidentalis*, was described by Dr. R.A. Philippi in 1873 in a German language paper titled "Ueber die Boa der westlichen Provinzen der Argentinischen Republik". The original specimens that were examined to describe this subspecies were from Cordillera in Mendoza and San Juan Provinces of Argentina. These boas were originally thought to be a color variant of *Boa constrictor* but later many significant differences were noted, especially in coloration. The snake used to describe this new subspecies (holotype) was a stuffed 7 foot 10 inch example from the vicinity of Mendoza. The original description went into great depth to describe this boa's appearance. Some of the attributes that Philippi described were as follows: The number of belly shields (ventral scales) amounts to 251, caudal plates (subcaudal scales) are 45. The nose is covered with approximately 30 plates; approximately 20 circle the eye, 21 are on each side of the upper lip, and 15 shields

stand in a diagonal line between the eyes. The rostral plate is somewhat taller in the *Boa* from Mendoza than in *B. constrictor*; and the chin plates differ only insofar as their margins are straight and not curved concavely. The foremost shield of the eye margin is in the same condition as in the Brazilian form. The coloration is conspicuously different and much darker than that seen in *Boa constrictor* and the belly is darkly spotted. The top of the head is also divided by a long brown stripe. The dorsum exhibits 28 body blotches or saddles from snout to vent and these are notched front and back with a lighter color in the center.

Boa c. orophias
St. Lucia Island Boa

The St. Lucia Island Boa, *Boa c. orophias*, was first described by Linneaus in 1758 as *Boa orophias*. He described this boa from St. Lucia as having 281 ventral scales which is the highest amount of ventrals compared to any of the other recognized subspecies today. Because of this high ventral scale count Dumeril and Bibron assigned this boa the name *Boa diviniloqua* in 1844 which is latin for "divine influence". In 1935 Stull combined both the Saint Lucian and Dominican Island boas under *constrictor orophias* and separated this composite from *constrictor* at the species level. At that time in history we must remember that there was not a lot of research being done on Boa and that these original descriptions were describing the St. Lucia boas as full species (not subspecies). It is still the opinion of some herpetologists today that these island boas are indeed speciating as this moment and evolution is taking place right in front of our eyes. It also is the strong opinion of some that these boas are indeed their own species *(Boa orophias)*. It wasn't until 1964 that James D. Lazell Jr. placed this boa into *Constrictor constrictor orophias* in a paper Titled "The Lesser Antillean Representatives of Bothrops and Constrictor". Lazell described this snake as a "Constrictor with a prominent snout and a convex canthus; 65 to 75 dorsal scale rows at midbody, 270 to 288 ventrals, and 27 to 31 distinct, subrectangular, dark dorsal saddles to the level of the anus; dorsal ground color rich brown; venter white with black or gray spotting pronounced".

Boa habitat in St. Lucia. Photo by Ricky Lockett.

Boa c. ortonii
Orton's Boa

Boa constrictor ortonii. Photo by Pablo Venegas Ibanez.

Boa c. ortonii was described by Edward Drinker Cope and was read before the American Philosophical Society in 1878. It was named in honor of Professor James Orton as he acquired a few of these boas during a trip to Peru in 1877. The type locality of this subspecies was from Chillette near Pacasmayo and the range of this boa was reported to be from Perico and the upper Maranon Valley to Piura and south to La Libertad in the arid region of northwestern Peru. *Boa c. ortonii,* (like the other subspecies) went through a few name changes in its herpetological history. In 1943 Schmidt and Walker named it *Constrictor constrictor ortonii.* And in 1951 Stimson classified it as what it is called today *Boa constrictor ortonii.*

Cope described these boas as being intermediate between *constrictor and imperator.* I find this interesting because both *constrictor* and *imperator* are separated by a geographic barrier, the Andes Mountains. These boas are basically genetically isolated from each other by a snow capped mountain range. This makes me believe that maybe there was a valley in the mountain range many thousands (if not millions) of years ago that opened for a short period of time and therefore a race of boa migrated west thru this valley to either hybridize with another form of boa or evolve into what it is today simply because of environmental conditions. This is simply a theory and there is no scientific proof. But Cope's observation is a valid one as *Boa c. ortonii* really does look like what would be the link between *imperator* and *constrictor*.

Cope studied two specimens to describe this new subspecies, an adult male from the state of La Libertad and an adult female from Chanchamayo in the state of Junin. Cope noted that the orbital scales were separated from the supralabials by a row of scales on both sides of the head and that Labial pits were not present. Cope though that this unique scalation distinguished this form from the other subspecies. The other scale counts were as follows. Dorsal scale rows of 57-72, ventral scales 243-253 and subcaudals 42-59. Cope also noted a dark median line on the head with a faint lateral projection between the eyes and that the overall coloration of this boa is light brown.

Boa constrictor sabogae
Pearl Island Boa

The Pearl Islands Boa was originally described by Thomas Barbour in 1906 in the "Bulletin of the Museum of Comparative Zoology". This paper was titled, "Vertebrata from the Savana of Panama". The original description name he used was *Epicrates sabogae*. He also compared this new subspecies to mainland Epicrates in his description as he was unaware at the time that it was indeed a Boa constrictor.

Barbour reported that two, four foot long specimens and one skin were collected from Saboga Island which is part of the Pearl Island archipelago off the southwest coast of Panama. He described it as a "rather dark reddish brown" snake and that its squamation (arrangement of scales), distinguish it from the mainland form (but he was referring to mainland *Epicrates*). He reported that the Saboga Island specimens had 65 and 67 mid body scale rows, the number of ventral scales were 242-247 and subcaudals scales numbered 49-70.

In 1946 Doris M. Cochran renamed this subspecies as *Constrictor constrictor sabogae* in a paper titled "Notes on the Herpetology of the Pearl Islands, Panama ". She examined six young and half grown specimens from San Jose (the second largest island in the Pearl Island archipelago). Her scale counts were as follows: Mid body scale rows 73-75, ventral scales 240-250, subcaudals scales 54-68, dorsal saddles snout to vent 20-23 and caudal blotches as 5-6. She described the dorsal saddles as being "Vinaceous-rufous to cinnamon and the tail as being vinaceous – rufous". The word "vinaceous" refers to the color of red wine and rufous is described as strong yellowish pink to moderate orange; reddish.

And finally in 1951, Lothar Forcart changed the name to *Boa constrictor sabogae*. The change was made in the scientific journal "Herpetologica" in an article titled "Nomenclature Remarks on Some Generic Names of the Snake Family Boidae". In this paper Forcart simply designated all the Boa subspecies to *Boa constrictor* from their past designation of *Constrictor constrictor.*

So as you can see this subspecies has seen a few name changes. However, there is no doubt that this is a valid taxon based on the fact that the Pearl Islands are 55 miles from the mainland of Panama, thus genetic isolation from the mainland is evident. The boas here have had 10 – 15,000 years to evolve as it was this amount of time that they separated from the mainland. True *Boa c. sabogae* are very rare in collections today. Their habitat, the Pearl Islands, are located 90 Kilometers (55 Miles) directly south of Panama City in the Bay of Panama. There are over 90 islands and 130 islets that make up the Archipelago de las Perlas (Pearl Islands). It was named by Balboa in 1513 because Buccaneers would hide out there to attack Spanish armadas laden with treasures. Isla Saboga or Saboga Island is located in the northwestern part the Archipelago and is quite small. The Islands are a tropical paradise with fresh water streams, white sand beaches and tropical rainforest with gentle sloping hills. Hurricanes are a rare occurrence in the Bay of Panama, thus rafting from island to island may not be as common as on the Caribbean side of Panama – However this rafting does occur thus some genetic mixing happens in this small archipelago.

Very few legal C.I.T.E.S. shipments of Boa have come from Panama in the past 10 years. I personally have seen only a handful of animals that are supposed *Boa c. sabogae*. I say "supposed", because the boas in the trade today have no provenance to the Pearl Islands. However, the boas I have seen do very much resemble and look like what Barbour and Cochran described. They also are identical to pictures that I have seen of boas from Saboga Island and pictured on Saboga Island. These boas are lean constrictors that look like they are more arboreal than ground dwellers. They have a very faint pattern (some are almost patternless) with a rust colored tail and faint saddles on a beige to orange background color. I would also note that they are naturally hypomelanistic with little to no black color or speckling and the bellies are completely clear white. They are very small boas and max out at around 5 feet. The eyes are gold or orange and very large. This feature is the most distinguishable feature of Island Boas in Panama. They have a faint-colored stripe behind the eye. This stripe is far more evident in mainland boas and this characteristic is yet another distinguishing feature of the island boas.

The wild-caught supposed *sabogae* that I have seen are fond of eating birds and do not have great appetites. In captivity they will eat rodents as well and seem to adapt to captivity quite well.

The scale counts that I have taken from 6 living supposed *Boa c. sabogae* specimens are as Follows: Mid body scale rows 74-75, ventral scales 249-25 0, subcaudals scales 55-65 and dorsal saddles snout to vent 21-22. These scale counts match exactly to what Cochran described from San Jose in the Pearl Islands. Therefore, it is very likely that these Boas are from an island that is either part of the Pearl Island Archipelago or an island that is in the Bay of Panama and is very close to the Pearl Islands (boas exists on most of the islands in the Bay of Panama). No one knows for sure where the boas we see now are from, but my educated guess is that they are definitely some type of island Boa. Hopefully with responsible breeding they will become more common in the future and their bloodline preserved.

C.I.T.E.S.

C.I.T.E.S. (the Convention on International Trade in Endangered Species of Wild Fauna and Flora) is an international agreement between Governments. Its aim is to ensure that international trade in specimens of wild animals and plants does not threaten their survival. C.I.T.E.S. was drafted as a result of a resolution adopted in 1963 at a meeting of members of IUCN (The World Conservation Union). The text of the Convention was finally agreed at a meeting of representatives of 80 countries in Washington DC., United States of America, on March 3rd 1973, and on July 1st 1975 CITES entered in force. The original of the Convention was deposited with the Depositary Government in the Chinese, English, French, Russian and Spanish languages, each version being equally authentic.

Colombian Boa. Photo by Nathan Hanks.

C.I.T.E.S. is an international agreement to which Countries adhere voluntarily. Countries that have agreed to be bound by the Convention (joined C.I.T.E.S.) are known as Parties. Although C.I.T.E.S. is legally binding on the Parties – in other words they have to implement the Convention – it does not take the place of national laws. Rather it provides a framework to be respected by each Party, which has to adopt its own domestic legislation to ensure that C.I.T.E.S. is implemented at the national level.

For many years C.I.T.E.S. has been among the conservation agreements with the largest membership, which currently includes 169 Parties.

Appendices I and II

1. Appendix I shall include all species threatened with extinction which are or may be affected by trade. Trade in specimens of these species must be subject to particularly strict regulation in order not to further endanger their survival and must only be authorized in exceptional circumstances. **Note;** there is only one boa subspecies that is Appendix I and that is *Boa c. occidentalis* from Argentina.

A captive-born Suriname Boa, *Boa constrictor constrictor*, available at a reptile show. Photo by Nathan Hanks.

2. Appendix II shall include all species which although not necessarily now threatened with extinction may become so unless trade in specimens of such species is subject to strict regulation in order to avoid utilization incompatible with their survival.

Note: All of the *Boa constrictor* subspecies are Appendix II animals.

Another way of looking at what C.I.T.E.S. is doing and how it works it to think of a C.I.T.E.S. document for a shipment of boas (imported or exported) as a Passport. This document is telling the country that is receiving the shipment that the boas were captive bred and born, captive born on a farm or taken from the wild without affecting the natural population that currently exists.

PHOTO GALLERY

Albino Boa.

Sunglow Albino Boa. Photo by Nathan Hanks.

Hypomelanistic Nicaraguan Boa.

Super Hypo Salmon Boa, *Boa constrictor imperator*.

Leopard Boa, *Boa constrictor imperator*.

Blood Boa, *Boa constrictor imperator*.

BIBLIOGRAPHY

Barker, David G. and Tracy M. Barker. 2006. Pythons of the World Vol. II, Ball Pythons: The History, Natural History, Care, and Breeding. VPI Library, Boerne, TX.

Daudin, Francois Marie. Histoire naturelle, generale et particuliere des reptiles: ouvrage faisant suite a l'histoire naturelle generale et particuliere, composee par Leclerc de Buffon, et redigee par C. S. Sonnini, member de plusiers societes savants. Paris, F. Dufart. (1801-1803). Vol. 5: 150.

Fitzinger. 1826. Neue Classification der Reptilien.

Forcart, Lothar. 1951. Nomenclature Remarks on Some Generic Names of the Snake Family Boidae. Herpetologica 7: 197-199.

Laurenti. 1768. Synopsin Reptillium.

Stejneger, L. 1901. An Annotated List of Batrchians and Reptiles Collected in the Vicinity of La Guaira, Venezuela, with Two New Descriptions of Snakes. Smithsonian Institution, U.S.N.M. Vol. XXIV(1248): 179-192.

Stull. O. G. 1932. Five New Subspecies of the Family Boidae. Occ. Pap. Boston Soc. Nat Hist. 8: 25-30.

Stull O.G. 1935. A checklist of the Family Boidae. Proc. Boston Soc. Nat. Hist. 40(8): 387-408.

Wegener.1966. The Origins of Continents and Oceans (4th edition). John Biram, translator. Dover Publications, Mineola, NY.

SUGGESTED READING

Barker, D. and T. Barker. 1994. Boas in the Spotlight. The Vivarium, 6(2): 38-41.

Bartlett, P. 2003. Red-tailed Boas and Relatives. Barrons. Hauppauge, NY.

Coote, Jon. 1993. The Boa Constrictor- Their Captive Husbandry and Reproduction. Practical Python Publications, Nottingham, U.K.

de Vosjoli, Philippe. 2004. The Art of Keeping Snakes. Herpetocultural Library. BowTie Press. Irvine, CA.

deVosjoli, Phillipe. 1990. The General Care and Maintenance of Red-tailed Boas. Advanced Vivarium Systems, Inc., Santee, CA.

deVosjoli, Phillipe, Klingengerg, Roger and Ronne, Jeff. 1998. The Boa Constrictor Manual. Advanced Vivarium Systems, Inc. Santee, CA.

Fogel, Dave. 1997. Captive Husbandry and Propagation of the Boa Constrictors and Related Boas. Krieger Publishing Co., Malabar, FL.

Freiberg, Marcos. 1982. Snakes of South America. T.F.H. Publications, Inc., Neptune City, NJ.

Mehrtens, John. 1987. Living Snakes of the World. Sterling Publishing Co., NY.

Rossi, J. 1996. What's Wrong With My Snake? Advanced Vivarium Systems, Inc. Santee, CA.

Tolson, Peter J. and Henderson, Robert W. 1993. The Natural History of West Indian Boas. R&A Publishing Limited, England.

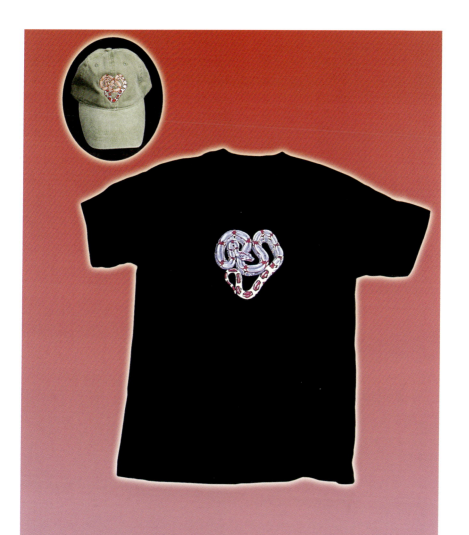